Working with Families of African Caribbean Origin

of related interest

Working with Ethnicity, Race and Culture in Mental Health
A Handbook for Practitioners
Hári Sewell
Foreword by Suman Fernando
ISBN 978 1 84310 621 0

Being White in the Helping Professions
Developing Effective Intercultural Awareness
Judy Ryde
Foreword by Colin Lago
ISBN 978 1 84310 936 5

Safeguarding Children from Abroad
Refugee, Trafficked and Migrant Children in the UK
Edited by Emma Kelly and Farhat Bokhari
ISBN 978 1 84905 157 6

Social Work, Immigration and Asylum
Debates, Dilemmas and Ethical Issues for Social Work and Social Care
Practice
Edited by Debra Hayes and Beth Humphries
ISBN 978 1 84310 194 9

Culture and Child Protection
Reflexive Responses
Marie Connolly, Yvonne Crichton-Hill and Tony Ward
ISBN 978 1 84310 270 0

Meeting the Needs of Ethnic Minority Children – Including
Black and Mixed Parentage Children
A Handbook for Professionals
2nd edition
Edited by Kedar Nath Dwivedi
ISBN 978 1 85302 959 2

Child Welfare Services for Minority Ethnic Families
The Research Reviewed
June Thoburn, Ashok Chand and Joanne Procter
Introduction by Beverley Prevatt Goldstein
ISBN 978 1 84310 269 4

Working with Families of African Caribbean Origin

Understanding Issues around Immigration and Attachment

Elaine Arnold
Foreword by Gill Gorell Barnes

Jessica Kingsley *Publishers*
London and Philadelphia

Appendix I, 'Map of The Carribbean', kindly provided by Kevin Robbins.

First published in 2012
by Jessica Kingsley Publishers
116 Pentonville Road
London N1 9JB, UK
and
400 Market Street, Suite 400
Philadelphia, PA 19106, USA

www.jkp.com

Library of Congress Cataloging in Publication Data
Arnold, Elaine, Ph. D.
  Working with families of African Caribbean origin : understanding issues
around immigration and attachment / Elaine Arnold ; foreword by Gill Gorell
Barnes.
      p. cm.
  Includes bibliographical references and index.
  ISBN 978-1-84310-992-1 (alk. paper)
  1. Immigrants--Services for--Great Britain. 2. Social work with immigrants-
-Great Britain. 3. West Indians--Great Britain--Social conditions. 4. West
Indians--Great Britain--Psychology. 5. Immigrants--Caribbean Area--Family
relationships. 6. Immigrants--Great Britain--Family relationships. 7.
Separation (Psychology) I. Title.
  HV4013.G7A76 2012
  362.84'96041--dc22
                              2011008152

British Library Cataloguing in Publication Data
A CIP catalogue record for this book is available from the British Library

ISBN 978 1 84310 992 1

Printed and bound in Great Britain

Contents

Foreword

This book is the culmination of a preoccupation that Elaine Arnold has had for some 40 years. I first met her in 1973 when she was a first year social work student at Sussex University, where I was teaching a course on Families and Child Care at the same time as working as a psychiatric social worker at Woodberry Down Child Guidance Clinic on the borders of the London boroughs of Hackney and Islington.

Elaine was already a qualified psychiatric social worker herself and changed her MSW (master's degree in social work) to an MPhil in order to research her first study of mothers whom she interviewed about their experiences of children whom they had left behind and who had subsequently rejoined them from the Caribbean, 'Out of Sight, Not Out of Mind'. Her work fitted some of the preoccupations of the clinic in those years, when we were trying to find methods of working with families, mainly Caribbean, whose children were having difficulty settling into primary school. This difficulty related to the hard lives their parents were having, based around long working hours and little time to play with or directly care for their children. The children in turn spent those long hours their mothers were working with child-minders who themselves often lived in over-crowded and under-stimulating conditions. The children were ill prepared for the concentration and learning required in primary school. At this time I was working with mothers in their own homes, and also sometimes with fathers, in school where their children went into intensive pre-school experience groups, known as Nurture Groups, for part of each school day or week.

Dr Arnold's work brought the wider perspective of the Caribbean migration into my thinking, and learning from her as we worked on planning her research, and in the wider context of reading all I could find written at that time, I have made awareness of Caribbean transition and the losses entailed part of my own professional life and thinking since

7

those days. While many people have written about the life transitions that migration involved (and the authors are widely referenced in this text), this book brings together all the different aspects of the story and places it firmly within the historical context of the islands where slavery and the deliberate separation of men, women and their children was part of the imposed structured economy for many generations.

I celebrate the arrival of this book because it is a testimony to the resilience of the human spirit surviving against sometimes terrible odds. It links the socio-historical dimensions of Caribbean family life with the importance of a psychological underpinning of attachment and commitment of family members to one another, for good mental health and a sense of identity. Dr Arnold gives testimony to the many ways in which families struggled to keep connections in the face of long absences and also looks at the cost for many mothers and children of their separation from one another.

In giving an account of slavery Dr Arnold charts a period of history that is painful and complex. For many years in the UK the black community were in disagreement as to whether taking slavery into account in thinking about their current life patterns did them disservice. Dr Arnold, taking the position that 'if one seeks to understand the social dynamics of today one must trace the major processes of history' (Manley 1974, p.45), looks at the power structure created, the parts played by white people and the roles created in those contexts for black people. For the purposes of this book history is framed to include the ways in which families, over generations, were subjected systematically to experiences of separation from one another; men were separated from their roles as providers for their family and holders of responsibility for their children; women were separated from intimate connection with partners; and all family members were seen as part of the units of production by the white plantation owners and their executives.

Children were trained to work from three years old and any thought about family, nurture and development had to be subsumed to economic and often brutally imposed principles in which black people were dehumanized for exploitative purposes. Dr Arnold links these experiences with subsequent family structures in which the principle of child-rearing was 'entrusted' by black people themselves to the larger 'family collective' as being a safer way of rearing children than the vulnerable single family. It was this long-held belief that children would be all right being raised by kin or the collective that 'allowed' mothers to believe that in leaving their children behind for many years while they came to work in the UK, their children would come to less harm.

Dr Arnold's mission has been to chart how this view, however initially generated and subsequently sincerely held, also came at a cost to the families involved. She has used attachment theory and the work devolving from John Bowlby's body of work (Bowlby 1940, 1952, 1965) on the effects on infants and children of early separation or prolonged separation from their primary caregivers, to explore the effects of separation and loss on Caribbean families who came to the UK from 1958 onward, leaving their children with relatives or neighbours. She explores the effects on mothers of being deprived of their children's 'growing' and the different attempts most of them made to show their children that they kept them 'in mind'. In her family interviews she describes how the effects of separation were ameliorated for children by continuing contact with their mother through letters, photos or parcels of clothing and food showing that they were kept in mind, but she also gives examples of how for many people this experience of separation was a lasting one of undermining and pain especially where the kin group did not bother to explain the mother's absence or were unkind or exploitative themselves.

Dr Arnold charts the experiences and misunderstandings that children and their parents had on reunification: non-recognition, feelings of alienation, feelings that their 'true' parents (their grandparents or aunts) had been left behind in the Caribbean, and on the children's side and on the parents' side feelings that these children who had now come over were not truly grateful for the suffering the parents had endured to give them a better life.

Dr Arnold also turns her attention to fathers in Caribbean families, challenging the stereotype that fathers were uninvolved parents by describing a number of different models of fathering in the families she interviewed as well as a number of different perceptions of the value of fathers voiced by mothers. Stepfathers too are valued for the time and attention they gave to children. The opinions voiced by children about fathers and stepfathers are similar in kind to those voiced in the 'Growing up in Stepfamilies' study (Gorell Barnes et al. 1997) of children reared in the UK and shows how similarity of pattern is found across different social and ethnic groups. One of the dangers in attributions about 'family style', or how members of families interact with each other, is that characteristics can be assigned as belonging to a particular ethnic group when they may more usefully be thought about as characteristics of family groups where certain life transitions have taken place.

Thus when the behaviours of mothers, fathers and children in this study are put within the wider lens of families worldwide who have suffered through loss and transition (whether through economic migration, or a result of war and enforced migration) patterns of loss and ambivalent reattachment can be found to be similar in shape and form, and not peculiar to the Caribbean family. The distinct additional legacy that the Caribbean family had to suffer from and triumph over is their earlier history of dislocation and enforced submission to patterns imposed on them by others; and it is the interactions between these two layered sets of losses and survival skills that this book alludes to and that need further consideration and piecing out even within the third generation in the UK today.

The evacuation of children in the UK during World War II (1939–1945) and the enforced emigration of children from this country to Canada and Australia also caused many children to be separated from their families for many years and this phenomenon of children experiencing separation from loved family is the background against which the studies of attachment and loss originally arose. However, it took many years for John Bowlby's ideas about the effects of separation on children to be accepted, perhaps particularly in a society and at a time when people had endured so much loss as a result of the world war.

My hope is that Dr Arnold's book will be received with greater readiness so that her thoughts about the implications for black children growing up in the UK today and the relevance of these legacies in their families can be put to good use, and create wider discussion between mothers, fathers and children as well as those who work with them.

Gill Gorell Barnes
Honorary Senior Lecturer, Tavistock Clinic, UK
and consultant family therapist

Acknowledgements

I would like to thank all of my colleagues, friends and students who have encouraged me to compile the research I have done over the years on the experiences of African Caribbean families and immigration. My thanks to Gill Gorell Barnes who persistently encouraged me to share my research about the immigration experience of African Caribbean families, and for writing the Foreword for the book.

I am deeply grateful to the many women who shared their memories of their lives in the Caribbean, and their separation and reunion experiences, and to the women and men who are members and supporters of the Separation and Reunion Forum, the organization founded as a result of my research in order to raise awareness of the phenomenon and its traumatic effects. My thanks to all those who helped in typing the manuscript and who read the drafts and made useful comments which helped to shape the book.

Preface

Over the years since researching the effects of broken attachments of African Caribbean families through separation and reunion during immigration to Britain, I have frequently been asked, 'When is the book coming?' Contributing to various journals and publications, and speaking to various voluntary groups, colleges and training organizations has kept me from devoting the time to compile the book until now.

What finally spurred me on was the repetition of debates of certain issues pertaining to African Caribbean people in Britain which were current in the 1970s and 1980s. Some of these are: the disproportionate numbers of African Caribbean boys under-achieving in schools, absent fathers, high numbers of children being looked after, the need to find black adoptive parents, black foster carers, transracial adoption, high incidence of mental illness and disproportionate numbers of black men in prison. I am also reminded that the history of the large scale immigration from the Caribbean is still not widely known when some indigenous people ask me, 'Why did African Caribbean people leave their countries with their lovely warm weather to live in Britain?'

The experiences of immigration were traumatic for a large number of families, who were not helped to mourn the loss of their families and all that was familiar and dear to them. However, it needs to be emphasized that grieving over broken attachments, separation and loss, and the need to mourn are not peculiar to African Caribbean families in Britain, nor do they only result from the experience of immigration. The process is common to individuals from all ethnicities, from all classes and across the life span who experience separation from families and all that is familiar to them through various circumstances.

When working with individuals who are unable to manage some of the challenges they encounter in their new surroundings, recognition of this is helped by knowledge of how individuals develop and the links between their early relationships, the internal models they have

of themselves and their expectation of the behaviour of others towards
them. Bowlby set out some of these concepts in his attachment theory,
and his seminal work continues to inspire research in the field of
sttachment, separation and loss.

This is not to suggest that social workers and therapists are able to
cure all the ills which beset people who feel afraid and insecure in their
environments. Sometimes there are very good reasons for these reactions
of individuals to their particular surroundings. Attention needs to be paid
to other factors, such as those resulting from policies, which impact on
the individual in negative ways, and workers in the helping professions
can be advocates for their clients.

Note: The names and personal details of the women who shared their
memories for the study have been changed in order to protect their
anonymity.

Introduction

This book places African Caribbean families in a historical context and draws together my earlier studies, the first of which examined the legacies of broken attachments, separation, loss and reunion of mothers and children of African Caribbean origins and the second of which considered whether the difficulties with which children had struggled when separated and subsequently reunited with mothers had persisted with them as adults.

My first study (Robertson 1975) was of African Caribbean mothers living in England who had separated from their children as a result of leaving them behind with extended families when they migrated. After varying periods of time, children were brought to Britain to be reunited with mothers, and in some instances, met new fathers/stepfathers and younger siblings. The evidence suggests that mothers who had been able to maintain contact during the separation through letters, photographs and visits were able to relate more successfully. Where mothers had not maintained ties, situations arose where they and their children were strangers to each other when they met, and several of them experienced unhappy reunions. What I sought to establish was evidence which would show that if mothers, in particular, had been prepared for the emotional reactions of the children and themselves which were likely to occur during the early periods of reunion, and had the mothers been helped to mourn their loss caused by separation from home and from their own mothers, they might have been better able to understand their children's separation anxieties, and consequently relationships could have been helped to be more satisfactory.

Sussex University supported my proposal to study the phenomenon of separation of African Caribbean mothers from their young children for long periods of time, and their subsequent reunion. The field work was carried out in two London boroughs where I was permitted to approach schools in order to access families, most of whom, when contacted, responded positively and were eager to discuss their experiences for the first time since their arrival in England.

The aims of the study were to document how mothers had reacted to the separation and reunion experiences and how they coped with living in a totally new environment, often in nuclear families and frequently as single parents. Equally important, the study attempted to explore the nature of the relationships between themselves and the reunited children. My aim was to listen to what they thought were contributory factors, and uncover their suggestions for ways in which they and the children could be helped. Because of my background in psychiatric social work I was interested in the impact of the social and cultural changes on the mental health of the mothers and I was also interested in the personality traits they possessed which might have influenced their relationships with others in general, and with their separated-reunited children specifically.

The second study (Arnold 2001) was undertaken at University College London, upon the suggestion of the late Jafar Kareem, founder of the Inter-Cultural Therapy Centre in London (founded in 1983). He had invited me to become involved in the work of the Centre having heard of my earlier study. Among the clients who attended were women who, as children, had been left in the Caribbean with extended families, who had been sent for later and whose reunions had resulted in unsatisfactory relationships. With Kareem's encouragement, I was prompted to research the phenomenon amongst a sample of women primarily because of their inability to make and sustain relationships with their mothers, partners, and in some instances with their children. This sample was contrasted with a control group of other women, with similar separation and reunion histories, who had adapted to the new situation of life in the reconstituted families satisfactorily. The aim was to uncover the factors which might have influenced the traumatic reunions and unsatisfactory relationships for some of the women and not others.

In the first and second studies outlined above, the theoretical base was attachment theory. I had become convinced through my experience, described below, and through studying some of the work of Bowlby (1952, 1982a), Ainsworth (1967), and other literature which addressed the phenomenon of broken attachment, separation and loss experienced by children and mothers, that the theory was applicable to the study of families from the Caribbean.

My experience was gained whilst teaching in a school on the site of a large 'orphanage' in Trinidad, which housed approximately 600 children. It was first established to house orphans of Indian immigrants who had died on the long journey from India to Trinidad during the nineteenth century. In time, children from a variety of backgrounds from among the African Caribbean population were admitted. Sometimes they were orphans, or abandoned babies, or children of young single mothers from financially deprived backgrounds whose families had rejected them as a result of becoming pregnant at early ages. Some of them were children of mothers in psychiatric hospitals or other hospitals with other illnesses, and some were of mothers who had migrated. Some children, aged seven or eight years, who were deemed beyond their mothers' control were also admitted.

Most of the families who were in abject poverty regarded placing the children in the institution as advantageous as their physical and educational needs would be met until they attained young adulthood. The mothers had no knowledge of the possible adverse effects on the social and emotional development of their children of separation at an early age from the continuous care of an individual and being cared for by a number of people working on a shift system.

The children were taught by trained teachers in a school situated within the grounds of the institution and vocational skills were taught by qualified staff. The carers on the other hand were untrained men and women, who insisted on blind obedience from the children, and who received neither training nor supervision to provide for the emotional needs of the children, particularly the younger ones.

It was very noticeable that when babies were admitted to the home and cared for in the nursery by a succession of carers who worked on shifts, they craved the attention of any adult who visited the nursery. They would raise their arms showing that they wanted to be held and those who were mobile attempted to seek close personal contact, apparently desperate for the comforting touch of an adult. Sometimes some of the babies 'failed to thrive'; they had poor appetites, did not grow or gain weight, and their milestones were retarded. They were cared for in the 'hospital' on the grounds which was staffed by a trained nurse, and where older girls were encouraged to visit and interact with the infants. The holding and close contact with their individual carers were beneficial to the babies, who showed some improvement in their development.

Children who were older and had experienced favourable family life before admission to the institution, and who were visited regularly by a parent or family member, were able to form satisfactory relationships with staff members and with their peers. They usually did well in school and some of them progressed to secondary and tertiary education. Some of the boys who had high levels of musical attainment were able to follow musical careers in the music bands of the army and of the police service.

Many of the younger children, however, exhibited disturbed behaviour and did not relate well with carers. They were disobedient, seeming not to hear when they were addressed, tended to be aggressive towards their peers, were inattentive in the classroom and so failed to achieve academically.

In an attempt to help some of the children experience life within families, the management introduced a scheme of inviting members of the community to assume the roles of 'uncles' and 'aunts' and these volunteers took the children into their homes to spend weekends and school holidays, and to celebrate birthdays and special occasions with their families. After regular contact with their surrogate families, these children showed marked development in their self esteem, communication skills and educational attainment. While some of these improvements may have been the results of the development of a sense of belonging to adults who were trustworthy and consistent, there were some children who did not have the opportunity to be placed in families and thus did not benefit from the experience of individual attention in a family setting.

On reaching adolescence those children whose families had maintained contact were able to return home if accommodation was available, whilst girls without families were placed as domestic workers in homes of middle-class families and boys in supervised after-care hostels. In time, social workers, probation officers, health and other welfare workers encountered some of the young adults as clients of the various services; most of the children had not been able to make and sustain relationships with anyone. A high proportion of the young women became single mothers, and in most instances were unemployed, and with little or no support from the fathers of the children, many of whom had also grown up in the institution, and were themselves unemployed. Some of these young mothers continued the cycle of placing their children in the institution, where they regarded the teachers and carers as surrogate extended families. Others struggled to cope for some time with independent living but the stresses and strains of poverty, and the lack of a supportive network within the community, took their toll upon their mental health and, in the absence of alternatives, some were admitted to the psychiatric hospital.

A number of the boys who had not been helped in working through their feelings of separation from and loss of their families whilst in the institution were never able to return to their original families and were placed in after-care hostels. These proved to be lonely places for them, having been reared in the communal environment of the institution, and some of the boys who lacked social skills reacted aggressively when in contact with others and invariably came to the attention of the police. Others, who found difficulty in obtaining employment, became involved in petty crimes and were detained in the 'Industrial School' (the equivalent of a detention centre) where some were able to further their education and acquire some useful vocational skills and were introduced to the world of work. Others continued to engage in anti-social behaviour and moved through the justice system, finally ending in prison (Lloyd and Robertson 1971).

The experience of teaching in the school of the institution and being involved in helping children deprived of family life to build their self esteem motivated my change of career from teaching to psychiatric social work, and I pursued a course at Manchester University, England, with a special interest in Child Guidance.

My work experience in placements as a social work student during the 1970s in various residential child care settings in England provided opportunities to observe the behaviours of the children and I found that these closely resembled the behaviours I had observed among African Caribbean children in the institution where I had worked in the Caribbean.

Over the years, in discussing with social care personnel some of the problems which brought families to the attention of their services, I found that their concerns were often about the high numbers of their clients who had experienced separation and loss through migration and the difficulties they were experiencing with their children, some having been left behind and reunited with their families after several years. Seldom was there an indication that the concepts of attachment theory were utilized to inform the workers' thinking in their work with those clients in order to enable them to unravel some of their feelings about their early experiences of separation and loss. It seemed that the concepts of attachment theory were not utilized generally in work with families, indigenous or migrant, in the 1970s. In recent years, especially in work with foster carers and with prospective adopters, the theory is explained in the preparation groups.

Although my research was concentrated on the mothers and the relationships with their children, this was not to ignore the roles which fathers played in the families, and mothers and children were given the opportunity to voice their opinions on the fathers, many of whom were present in their families at the time. Some fathers had accepted responsibilities in helping with caring for the children and engaging with them positively and the families functioned well but there were instances when men lived up to the stereotype of being absent from the home.

I believe that it is necessary to understand the history of the past experiences of serial immigration of African Caribbean families. Unsatisfactory reconstituting of many, and the seeming transgenerational trauma, have impacted adversely upon the lives of many children and impeded progress in their development, educationally, socially and economically.

There is a need to consider other factors within the family, such as unfair treatment, favouritism, physical, sexual and emotional abuse, and also factors in the wider society. There may be racism and other forms of hostility from members of the dominant ethnic group directed at the individual, the family, or the ethnic group to which the family belongs. Government policies may not facilitate the provision of essential amenities and services which make it possible to care for families in ways that are conducive to the establishing of satisfactory relationships within the family, in the workplace or in the wider community.

All those who work with families (not only of African Caribbean origin, but of all ethnicities) seeking help with problems are in prime positions to help them to recognize and reflect upon some of the factors of their early experiences which may be contributing to their present states of mind, and also to consider whether they can be advocates to effect changes which may help to remove some of the stumbling blocks which prevent them and their families from living more comfortable lives.

The book contains seven chapters arranged as follows:

- Chapter 1 gives a historical overview of African Caribbean family structures and considers how much of the slave and plantation culture has been retained. It goes on to look at the place of women and men within the family, the care of children, the values of religion and work, attitudes to race and colour, and reactions to authority, to discrimination and to racism.

- Chapter 2 gives an overview of the African Caribbean immigration to Britain. It looks at the circumstances in which they lived, the lack of policies and provisions by the various governments, discrimination, and immigration laws which made life difficult for the immigrants.

- Chapter 3 provides a brief description of attachment theory, the theoretical basis of the studies.

- In Chapter 4 some mothers recall their feelings about separation from their children. When they came to Britain, these mothers left their children in the care of the extended family. They also recall their feelings on reunion with their children.

- Chapter 5 considers the fathers in the studies: how they were viewed by partners and by children.

- Chapter 6 gives a summary of the reunification of families in Britain, experienced by children, now adults.

- Chapter 7 considers what has changed for contemporary African Caribbean families, and the implications for current work. It also gives suggestions for future research.

Chapter 1

A Brief Historical Background of African Caribbean People

> There are many who would prefer to console themselves by suggesting that it is bad to dwell in the past. Certainly I would concede that one must not take up permanent residence in the past. However, if one seeks to understand the social dynamics of today, one must trace the major processes of history. (Manley 1974, p.45)

Debates on the origins of African Caribbean people and the effects of slavery continue over the years, not only among professionals but also lay people, some of whom question the relevance of the past to contemporary society, as the quotation above from Manley (1974) demonstrates.

The backgrounds of migrants who came from the Caribbean to Britain are extremely complex, and among the host community there have been some misconceptions based on the belief that the migrants came from a homogenized region of the Caribbean and that they were all of one ethnic group. This last misconception may have arisen because of the large numbers of those of African Caribbean origin who arrived together; but there were also families from the Caribbean who were of Indian, Chinese or European origins, and of mixed heritage, though in smaller numbers. These are seldom seen as clients of the social services.

The migrants who came from the islands and the two mainland territories of the Caribbean region which were British colonies were called 'West Indians'. Recently, many black people in Britain have chosen to be called 'African Caribbean', since they were not descendants of the indigenous people so named by Christopher Columbus in 1492, but were descendants of Africans taken by Europeans to the Caribbean as slaves. Columbus was one of the many explorers from Spain and Portugal 'caught up in the "discovery mania" in the fifteenth century' (Beckles and Shepherd 2004, p.33). He was convinced that by sailing west he would arrive in the East to gain access to the wealth of Asia. Sighting land in the Atlantic, Columbus believed that he was nearing Asia, and that he had arrived in the neighbourhood of India; since he had done so by sailing west from Spain, he called the islands the West Indies.

The islands named the West Indies are found in the archipelago which extends from the tip of Florida in North America to within seven miles of the coast of Venezuela in South America. The right of possession of the new territories was granted to Spain by the Pope in 1494. In 1496 the first permanent Spanish settlers envisaged an economy based on mining for gold, but there were only meagre findings which were not lucrative and the industry was replaced in the sixteenth century by agriculture with the cultivation of cotton, tobacco and sugar cane requiring intensive labour. The Europeans tried to enslave the indigenous groups of people, namely two tribes of the Amerindians, Arawaks and Caribs, but they were considered not strong enough for the intensive labour required in the industry; many succumbed to diseases, both tropical diseases and those transmitted by the Europeans and against which they had no immunity. Many resisted the Europeans but were finally defeated and were transported to Central America; a small number settled in the rain forest of Dominica (Beckles and Shepherd 2004). There are people in some of the other islands such as St Lucia, Dominica and Trinidad who claim Carib heritage.

Following the explorations of Spain in the Caribbean region, other European powers became interested in searching for gold, and in succeeding centuries, England, France, the Netherlands and Denmark fought to dominate the region, taking territories by force or default and trading them to settle accounts. During the sixteenth, seventeenth and eighteenth centuries their various cultures influenced language, male–female relationships, family structures, child-rearing practices, and attitudes to race and colour, and so created considerable diversity among the populations.

By the end of the nineteenth century, the islands were no longer traded back and forth among the European powers. Those which were acquired by the English stayed in their possession for another three hundred years, until most of them became independent during the 1960s with only a few of the smaller islands, Montserrat, Turks and Caicos, remaining under British rule (Williams 1964).

The islands claimed by the English included Jamaica, which is situated within the group of larger islands known as the Greater Antilles. The smaller islands further east in the chain are subdivided into the Leeward Islands which comprise Antigua, Barbuda, St Kitts, Nevis, Anguilla and Montserrat; and the Windward islands consisting of Grenada, St Lucia, St Vincent and Dominica. The Turks and Caicos Islands, the Caymans, the Virgin Islands and the Bahamas are the most northern, Barbados the most easterly; Guyana is in the north of South America, and Belize in the eastern part of Central America (see Appendix 1).

During the early days of British colonization, in the Caribbean region, English land-owners imported white labourers from Britain. They were chosen from among a variety of people such as poor white servants indentured for three to seven years, convicts sent to serve for a specific length of time, people working off large debts or those who had offended the government on political or religious grounds. Nevertheless, there were insufficient free labourers to be obtained for the intensive cultivation of sugar cane, tobacco and cotton. The system of slavery, which forced people to work for long hours and for little reward, was considered by the colonists to be the solution.

Like the Portuguese before them, the English turned to Africa, a large and diverse continent, and transported millions of people whom they bought or captured. According to Beckles and Shepherd (2004) the transatlantic slave trade first centred on West, Central and Southern Africa but to meet the demands for slaves the traders proceeded to the eastern coast. However, it is commonly believed that the majority of slaves taken to the Caribbean were from West Africa, and Davison (1962) affirmed that in the New World, in spite of the slaveholders' efforts to subdue the slaves, the Africans were often strong and numerous enough to revive and recreate the customs, beliefs and practices of their homelands. The atrocious conditions under which slaves were obtained and taken from Africa, the horrors of the journey across the Atlantic ocean and the cruel treatment meted out to slaves on the plantations have been documented by historians such as Williams (1964), Patterson (1967), Hogg (1979) and Beckles and Shepherd (2004).

Williams (1964) expressed the view that the treatment of African slaves by the plantation owners was patterned on the treatment which was meted out to their white servants and labourers: 'The felon-drivers in the plantations became without effort, slave-drivers' (Williams 1964, p.19). However, the major difference was that the white labourers had been indentured for a limited period of time after which they were free to do what they pleased. The slaves were 'property' bought for life, and their status was passed on to their children. Williams refuted the myth that manual work and the climate in the Caribbean were too stressful for white labourers. White workers had laboured in Barbados, where dissidents were sent by the British government for more than a hundred years, and Williams concluded that a racist ideology that black people were inferior was the justification for their enslavement.

Most of the slaves were not passive victims; they resisted in their own countries when they were being captured, on board ships, during the transatlantic journey, and they revolted on the plantations across the Caribbean region. According to Beckles and Shepherd (2004) many ran away and became known as Maroons in the countries wherever there were hiding places, and where these were not available some took to the sea. The best known of the Maroons were those who established themselves in the rain forests of the Dutch colony of Surinam in South America, and those in the mountainous areas of Jamaica. English armies sent out to recapture the latter were defeated repeatedly. After several years of war, peace was negotiated and the Maroons were left to live free from interference. One well-known leader of the Maroons in Jamaica was a woman known as Nanny. She is considered the most outstanding woman of the eighteenth century, 'leading her people with courage and inspiring them to maintain that spirit of freedom, that life of independence which was their rightful inheritance' (Ellis 1986, p.27).

The more slaves demonstrated that they were not passive victims, the more fearful the slave-owners became and so they introduced more repressive laws. Michael Manley, a former Prime Minister of Jamaica, expressed the view that the slave-owners had instituted policies with the aim of destroying the cultural and social systems which the slaves had taken with them from their homelands. When emancipation was achieved, the individuals evolved with new attitudes and new needs. For example, in Jamaica, the freed slaves carried with them the distrust of authority and many established their own farming settlements scattered over the mountains as far away as possible from the sugar plantations where they had been enslaved. Those who remained to work on the plantations succumbed to the authority of the owners since, in the absence of an institution of their own, they had no choice:

> Nevertheless they retained a lingering resistance to the idea of authority which expressed itself in opposition to any form of regimentation, and in resentment to discipline. In this, the Jamaican shares a common experience with his brothers throughout the Caribbean, and indeed with all people whose present attitudes reflect a collective recollection of tyranny. (Manley 1974, pp.28–9)

WEST INDIAN FAMILY STRUCTURES

Many theorists have speculated upon the origins of the organization of the West Indian family, and have asked whether it is a survival of slavery, of African forms of family, of early European forms, or whether it developed from the pressures of the plantation society and colonialism.

Sociologists and anthropologists have written in detail about the background of the West Indian society and formations of the family; some of them are household names such as Edith Clarke (1966), M.G. Smith (1965), R.T. Smith (1956, 1988) and Lowenthal (1972).

THE FAMILY UNDER SLAVERY

Little regard was paid to the keeping of families together when the Africans were taken from their countries where their culture revolved around family life. When they arrived in the New World, couples, parents and children were often separated and sold to various plantation owners. A personal testimony of children being separated from their mother and sold several times was that of Mary Prince (Hogg 1979). She was extremely resilient, and rebelled against the ill treatment meted out to her and married against the master's permission. Some 30 years after having been sold as a child, she was taken to England to take care of the children of her slave-owner, and realising that she was a free woman in England she was determined that the English people should hear at first hand what a slave felt about their loss of freedom and their suffering at the hands of those who withheld freedom from them. Mary Prince obtained the help of a philanthropist and wrote her autobiography (1831), and she rose to prominence in the anti-slavery political movement in London (Beckles and Shepherd 2004).[1]

The number of African slaves in the various colonies increased through importation and also by natural means, but in the early days slaves were not considered as possessing emotional feelings to kin nor commitment to family values. It is alleged that the male slaves were used for breeding in similar fashion to livestock, and the bearing of responsibility by a father could only be regarded as a distraction. When occasionally a man was able to provide food for his family from the land he was permitted to cultivate, this was dependent on the goodwill of the slave master and therefore he could not regard himself nor be regarded by his family as the provider (Simey 1946). The slave-owners considered family life among the slaves as 'an irrelevant, unimportant and sometimes criminal institution' (Beckles and Shepherd 2004, p.150).

However, some slave-owners, anxious to have newcomers adapt to the work on the plantations, utilized the culture of the society from which the slaves had come to their advantage and placed newly arrived slaves with older selected 'tutors' of similar ethnic backgrounds. According to Edwards (1793, quoted by Hogg 1979), the older people were pleased to receive their young country folk, and they were given the task of preparing them for work on the plantations; this was called 'seasoning'. The newcomers were pleased with the arrangements and considered themselves to be the adopted children of those older persons, whom they called 'parents' and from whom they received protection. This arrangement had favourable outcomes for the newcomers who, when well treated and free from physical illnesses, became reconciled to the country and well established in their 'families', thus proving to be as valuable as those who were born in the country.

Women worked in the fields alongside the men and those who became mothers were compelled to resume work shortly after the birth of their children. On large plantations, mothers who breast-fed their babies were allowed to carry them tied on their backs (as was the custom in Africa) to the fields (Hogg 1979), but generally, children were regarded as the property of the slave master, and were assigned to the care of older women no longer physically able to work. These carers were not

---

1   A plaque in her honour was unveiled during the commemoration of the abolition of the transatlantic slave trade (2007) on a building where she lived, situated on the site of the Senate House of the University of London.

expected to nurture the children but to train them from as early as three years old for their future tasks in the fields (Hogg 1979).

The church assisted with efforts at stimulating reproduction by offering special dispensations to mothers, to overseers, or managers of the plantations, but never to fathers. For example, mothers were offered a period of leave from work after giving birth, as well as cash for producing healthy babies, and premiums were paid to overseers and managers who were able to account for a natural increase of slaves on the plantations. Massiah (1982) concluded that the practice gave legitimacy to the centrality of the role of mothers, which was accepted in the family system of the people of West African origin who had been taken to the New World.

When the transatlantic slave trade was abolished (1807) and it became more difficult to obtain slaves from Africa, some slave-owners considered it to be in their best economic interest to encourage stable families and better care of the children, and some couples were allowed to live as nuclear families, whilst others lived in households of mothers and their children.

Braithwaite (1959) warned that there was a tendency to speak of the West Indian family too loosely. He claimed that even under slavery, family life was differentiated with a sharp distinction between house and field slaves. Henriques (1973) also spoke of the difference in the rearing of children. Some slave-owners allowed the children who were the progeny of themselves and African slave women to live in the plantation houses (Henriques 1973). These children were in a position to know their fathers and to be known by them but no information could be found as to how much interaction there was between fathers and children. Some of the women accepted the arrangements, which safe-guarded their children from the harsh conditions of field labour and mistreatment, but others resisted the bearing of children who inherited their slave status. According to Beckles and Shepherd (2004) slave-owners offered money to women to produce healthy babies, and to midwives for delivering them, but the managers found it difficult to understand why the birth rates were low and why there was a high rate of infant deaths. Infanticide was not uncommon as the women's way of protest, and their opposition to slavery.

SOCIAL STRUCTURE

As a direct result of the use of black slave labour, the divisions of the society in the West Indies were based not only on class and wealth, but also very prominently on skin colour (Dookhan 1971). Because of the mating patterns of white slave-owners with black slaves and those of mixed heritage with white and black partners, over the years, many variations of skin colour, racial features and hair formation emerged among the population. These differences assumed importance in the society, the structure of which became one of a colour/class pyramid (see Figure 1.1), but this simplified description reveals nothing of the complexity of the status and lifestyles of the people.

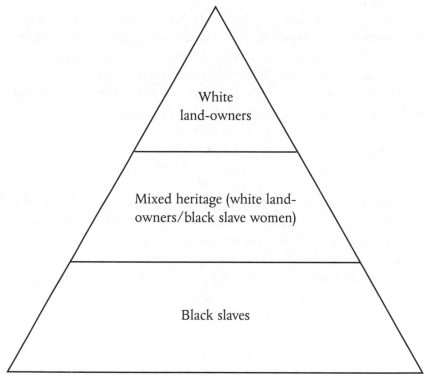

Figure 1.1 Colour/class pyramid of West Indian society

The white planters owned and administered everything, but many tended to live in their mother countries, for example in England. The administrators who represented their interest in the colonies were at the apex of the pyramid. Next in the hierarchy were those of mixed heritage, the progeny of Europeans and black women who were born free or who were able to acquire their freedom: they were thus 'Free People of Colour' (Beckles and Shepherd 2004; Hearne and Nettleford 1963) and whilst they enjoyed fewer privileges than the whites, they were not chattel. Freedom was extended to some slaves by their owners and they eventually joined the ranks of a coloured population (Braithwaite 1971). At the bottom of the pyramid were the black labouring class who were graded according to shades of skin colour with those with the darkest complexion at the base of the pyramid.

Black people outnumbered everyone else and suffered the greatest disadvantages. Lighter skin colour became the criterion of selection for employment and this was especially so among the women. This pyramidical structure continued in Caribbean societies for several decades after the emancipation of slavery, and discrimination against people of darker skin colour was blatant in the workplace. The preference for those of lighter skin colour was demonstrated in social life and black men often selected women of lighter skin colour to be their wives: when they studied abroad they often returned with a white partner from the country in which they studied (Henriques 1953; Richmond 1961). Children in families were also rated in preference by their skin colour, with the fair-skinned ones being described as the pretty ones.

ILLEGITIMACY

The majority of slaves were taken to the New World from West Africa, which was a peasant culture. The man who possessed a large number of wives and children obtained the greatest assistance in farming. Socially the polygamist was regarded as wealthy and his prestige rose with the number of wives, and the wives enjoyed his high reputation (Ojike 1946). The legitimacy of his children by his numerous wives would not be held in question since through his wealth he would have made the necessary payments which established their legality.

Davison (1962) holds the view that the Africans in the New World were often strong and numerous enough to revive and recreate the customs and beliefs of their homelands, and Starobin (1974) states that though family life was strained by forced separations, this was not allowed to strip the Africans of their distinctive culture.

Some of the slaves were elevated to responsible positions on the plantations and, as head men, they continued the custom of polygamous mating; they could maintain two or more wives, and their children were not regarded as illegitimate (Patterson 1967).

In the countries where the Anglican denomination was prominent there was a reluctance on the part of the slave-owners to convert the slaves to Christianity which advocated monogamy. However, missionaries, especially from among the Methodists and Moravian churches, converted some of the slaves and tried to promote marriages, but monogamous marriages were not always sustained (Beckles and Shepherd 2004), and men often fathered children outside of the marital home. The status of these children was illegitimate.

An opinion often expressed when debating the phenomenon was that slaves emulated the customs of the plantation owners who engaged in the practice of fathering illegitimate children outside of their marital home (Hearne and Nettleford 1963).

The emancipation of the slaves did not increase the practice of marriage, as poverty remained constant and a man would refuse to marry until he was able to provide a home for a wife who was considered to be worthy of a high standard of living. Some men who were fathers or stepfathers of their children maintained a visiting relationship with the family while many women headed households and bore the full responsibility of caring for the children.

In a survey of West Indian family structure, M.G. Smith (1962) drew attention to the writings of two well-known American writers, namely Franklin Frazier (1953), a black American sociologist from Chicago, and Melville Herskovits (1966). They argued that black families in the Caribbean and the USA were distinctive in their high rates of marital instability, high rates of illegitimacy and high numbers of maternal households. Herskovits argued that these patterns were of African derivation, whilst Frazier highlighted the influences of the different social and economic contexts of the families. He pointed out that among the black middle-class professionals, marriage was the norm of family life and illegitimacy was rare, whilst among rural black families in the southern states of America, maternal families and illegitimacy were common and the rates of marriage were relatively low. This thesis was applicable to Jamaica and other West Indian societies, where illegitimacy, maternal families and co-habitation were, according to the statistics, the patterns of life of the lower socio-economic groups (Henriques 1953; Simey 1946).

Smith (1956), writing of family life in Guyana, described the young man's tie to his mother and showed him contributing money to her support. This tie was not easily broken with him continuing to live at home with her even when he might have fathered several children, thus leaving the responsibility for the children's care and maintenance to the mothers.

Clarke (1966), researching in Jamaica, referred to some young men's attachment to their mothers who, she claimed, impressed upon them that it was their duty to compensate for the hardships the mothers had endured as their sole or principal support during their early lives. This attachment to the mother on the part of many young men usually hindered the formation of stable relationships as the men refused to leave the homes of their mothers until after their deaths. Clarke, studying three different communities in Jamaica, showed that the attitudes to marriage and other forms of unions differed in the various communities, but that in all of the relationships, the women were required to remain faithful to their partners, while this requirement was not made of the men. This could be said of all communities in the region.

There has been a considerable amount of discussion about illegitimacy among African Caribbean people over the decades, and it has become acceptable among consensual unions, but the argument that legitimacy or illegitimacy does not matter among people of the Caribbean was refuted by Braithwaite (1959). He argued that the discrepancy between legitimacy and illegitimacy represented a real split in the society between children born to legally married parents and those born to unmarried mothers, and has at times presented serious problems regarding the inheritance of property if the father who had shared the family home with his partner, regarded in common law as his wife, died intestate. If paternal relatives so wished, they were entitled to the estate of the deceased.

This unjust practice continued through the years in the Caribbean countries until the 1970s when Barbados and Jamaica took the lead in reforming the law relating to family matters. One of the significant changes was to grant equal legal status to all children through the Status of Children Act (1976) (see Forde 1981). However, the legality of a situation does not necessarily confer a feeling of belonging and self worth on children who are not considered to be of as high a status as those born to married parents.

MARRIAGE

Henriques (1953) and Green (1973) drew attention to the tendency of researchers of the African Caribbean family to exclude studies of middle-class families where the 'Christian family' was based on marriage and the dominance of the father.

Many stable unions among working-class couples, especially those living in rural areas, tended to culminate in marriage when the children were grown and the economic situation became more stable. Marriage therefore seemed to correlate with an improvement in economic status. Blake (1961) held the opinion that most Jamaican women of the lower classes desired marriage and approved of marital union as the preferred form of men and women living together based on Christian teaching. Blake drew attention to the increasing number of marriages as women grew older. Blake's view seems to be worthy of some consideration with regard to the unmarried among early African Caribbean immigrants, many of whom married on arrival in Britain. Several factors may have contributed to this, such as the need for companionship in the absence of the extended families, increased earnings, income tax concessions for married couples, and the improved status acquired by legal marriage.

RELIGION

The Roman Catholic Church was the first to establish a foothold in the New World, when a Spanish priest who accompanied Columbus in 1493 landed on West Indian soil and gave it his blessing (Dookhan 1971). Subsequently when the British entered the region, the Anglican and other Christian denominations, such as Methodist, Moravians, Baptists and Quakers, followed. The church became involved in the owning of slaves, but whereas the Spaniards considered it an opportunity to convert heathens, the British planters were reluctant to introduce slaves to Christianity for several reasons. According to Williams (1964), it was thought that the slaves would become less docile and conforming, and that being taught in the English language would allow the various tribes to master a common language, thus enabling them to plot rebellion. The planters were also reluctant to reduce the working week by allowing Sundays off for attendance at church. During the eighteenth century, missionaries of the non-conformist churches, especially the Moravian, Wesleyan and Baptist churches, were active, but were instructed by the plantation owners to impress upon the slaves that their position had been willed by God, and that in order to be saved from suffering in hell fire eternally, they needed to perform their tasks well (Beckles and Shepherd 2004).

The slaves retained the beliefs they brought with them, some of which assisted their survival and helped them to endure their hardships with the hope of a better life after death. These sentiments were expressed in some of the spiritual songs especially composed by slaves in North America. Some of these, rearranged by prominent musicians, are performed in contemporary society by musicians across racial groups (Hogan 2001).

The African connection was not entirely broken by the missionaries. Hearne and Nettleford (1963) claimed that the slaves in Jamaica had only a vague and uncertain connection with orthodox Christianity, and were not encouraged to feel that the accepted forms of worship were of importance or relevance to them. (It is interesting to note the similar attitudes of the established Church to African Caribbean immigrants when they first arrived in Britain.)

When the slaves were denied full participation in Christian practices they evolved their own forms. They selected from Christianity what pleased them, and what they considered useful in providing them protection, and blended them into their forms of worship. This mixture has given rise to a number of different sects which, although they carry Christian titles and use the Bible, are different from the rituals of the orthodox. 'The Europeans' religion was never adopted in its entirety by most Jamaicans; in many cases it was transformed…above all Christianity never uprooted the pagan superstitions to which the great majority of Jamaicans still subscribe' (Hearne and Nettleford 1963, p.29). One of these, known as 'obeah' (a mixture of belief in and use of the supernatural), is common in all of the islands and many people, even those devoted to the Christian Church, tend to believe in its magical powers.

After emancipation, the church and the schools provided by religious bodies were influential in Europeanizing the Africans and their descendants who accepted the process, recognizing the economic and social advantages. Then as now, not all found total satisfaction in orthodox Christian worship. It seemed that the revivalist forms of religion were more satisfactory not only in meeting their spiritual needs, but also in providing places where a sense of belonging was experienced by those of the lower socio-economic levels of the society, and a place where they were able to express themselves more freely in song and dance. They also provided opportunities for leadership from among the black population and the expression of talents in administration, public speaking, teaching and music.

In the twentieth century, a distinct form of religion, Rastafarianism, emerged in Jamaica and spread to other West Indian islands. Its founders rejected a white God and deified Haile Selassie, late emperor of Ethiopia. They found inspiration in the words of the Old Testament of the Bible which they proffered in explanation of wearing their hair in locks, smoking of 'ganja' (cannabis) and of their general beliefs and lifestyle. They venerated Marcus Garvey who 'was a beacon of Black enlightenment at a time when White supremacy saw nothing good about the African and many Creoles disavowed the African part of their heritage' (Thomas 2008, p.14). Marcus Garvey proposed his ideology that black people should return to Africa, but this was impossible and out of touch with reality since the black people of the Caribbean were uncertain of their places of origin. Besides the difference in cultural norms of those from the Caribbean and the Africans, there were practical considerations, such as financing the return, accommodation and employment.

Whereas the slaves envisaged a beautiful life in 'heaven', the Rastafarians' hope was to return to their homeland free and having salvation (Morrish 1971). In both instances, religion was considered to be a means of improving their survival.

CONCLUSION

The celebrations marking the bicentenary of the abolition of the transatlantic slave trade in Britain during 2007 were the catalyst for many debates and discussions in various circles about the long-lasting impact of slavery on African Caribbean people. In conversations with a number of women in the age range of 32–50 I asked their views on the effects of slavery on their parenting. Some responses were:

> 'I was taught about slavery at school, as a historical fact. We did not dwell on it. It did not make any difference on how I brought up my children, the best I could.' (Mrs S, age 40)

> 'I am bringing up my two children as I was brought up, in a home with two parents, never mind that my father was not

too energetic in the home, but he always worked hard, but my mother kept the home going.' (Mrs R, age 38)

'I am bringing up my daughter the best way I know – loving her, talking with her. Somehow it seems that slavery made a bigger impact on some men and they cannot commit themselves to accepting responsibility for a family.' (Miss D, age 32)

'I know slavery was horrible, but now there is no time to sit down and worry about it. Sometimes I think some people use it as an excuse instead of trying hard to make life better for themselves and their families.' (Ms C, age 38)

The sample is evidently too small to draw general conclusions about how women in contemporary society feel about the influence of slavery upon their form of living, but the interviewees were clear in expressing their views that in spite of their history, it is now their responsibility to care for their children and prepare them to live in present-day society, not to dwell on the past and lose opportunities that are open to them in the present.

I know from discussions with colleagues that some of them believe that the collective memory of the devastating experiences of slavery of the ancestors of the population of African origin in the Caribbean, has left lasting emotional scars through the generations and that some people have been left regarding themselves perpetually as victims. I am among those who do not deny the historical facts of our ancestry, but believe that it is necessary to move on from attributing blame for every inability to achieve one's aims as due to the person's history of being a descendant of slaves. People in this contemporary society need to recognize when racism is being used to block their progress, and to challenge this. They also need to be able to accept responsibility for their actions and examine the contribution they themselves make to obstructing their progress.

Many African Caribbean people in spite of their ancestry have progressed in various professions and have had outstanding careers in Britain. They have been resilient and notwithstanding adverse circumstances such as poverty, racism, emotional and/or physical ill health, they have cared for their families and have made important contributions to their communities and to the wider society. Unfortunately, in some other cases, parents have seen their children reject their strong work ethic, and become dependent on the welfare system, others living within a drug culture which fosters dependence. In some instances the craving for the drugs leads to other crimes which brings the individuals into conflict with the law. The lack of educational success of their children is a great disappointment for parents as one of their reasons for immigrating was to see their children move from grinding poverty and be successful in their lives through education.

Immigration from the Caribbean to Britain is discussed in the following chapter.

Chapter 2

Immigration of African Caribbean People to Britain

> Circulation of workers from one point of an island to another
> and among islands as well as great migration to cities, testifies
> to the glorious appeal of seeking opportunities, limited though
> they be in a free society. (Pearcy 1965, p.64)

Many Caribbean people have migrated internally and externally in
order to escape the trap of poverty and, according to Pearcy (1965), this
testifies to the appeal of seeking opportunities wherever they occurred.

The rapid growth in the number of black people (i.e. with one or both
parents conventionally regarded as black) in Britain after World War II
(1939–1945) confirmed the impression held by many indigenous people
that the presence of black people in Britain was a new phenomenon.
This was a misconception; according to Alexander and Dewjee (1981)
black people had settled permanently in England since about 1555, but
this was seldom spoken of. More well known and commented upon was
that through the practice of slavery, in some white households during
the seventeenth and eighteenth centuries, it was fashionable to possess
black servants. Some of these were taken directly from Africa by some
captains of ships, or by plantation owners from the Caribbean. It was
estimated that in the eighteenth century there were 14–20,000 black
people in the population of 750,000 in London.

Besides those in slavery and in service, there were free black people,
some of whom had bought their freedom, whist others had been
rewarded by their owners with the granting of freedom for faithful
service. The numbers were increased through the birth of children, and
with those who fled from the West Indies and those who worked on ships

from North America after the American War of Independence (1776) and landed at various British ports. Many of them worked as domestic servants and were paid wages similar to those of the white domestics, and were free to change their jobs if they so wanted. Some black people were apprenticed to artisans and traders, but because of severe competition for apprenticeships they were often given poor working conditions and pay (Alexander and Dewjee 1981).

After the emancipation of the slaves, many freed slaves in England who chose to leave the households of the aristocracy tried to live independently but often found this impossible due to lack of employment at their trades; some were beggars on the streets, especially in London, but others returned to the Caribbean as free labourers.

There were some black people who became socially mobile with the help of rich patrons and members of the nobility. For example, in the eighteenth century Francis Williams, son of a freed slave from Jamaica, was sent to Cambridge University where he studied literature, Latin and mathematics after which he gained access to fashionable Georgian society and was remembered as 'an able poet'. There were other notable black people of American and African backgrounds.

Some children of mixed heritage from the West Indian colonies were sent by their fathers to England to be educated. Some of them inherited wealth from their fathers, who owned plantations and businesses, and were accepted into fashionable homes. Thackeray wrote of one such heiress in his 1847 novel *Vanity Fair*.

It is alleged that by the middle of the nineteenth century, there was a high incidence of intermarriage between black men and white English women. Also by the end of the century significant black communities had grown up around Britain's ports as seamen, seldom accompanied by women, settled in Liverpool, Cardiff, Bristol, Hull and London with partners/wives and their children.

The numbers of black people rose when they came to Britain to serve during World War I (1914–1918) and some of them settled in England (Alexander and Dewjee 1981).

Between the two world wars, several middle-class families in the Caribbean and some African countries, such as Nigeria and Ghana, sent their children to Britain to be educated, and governments sponsored numbers of students to attend British universities such as Oxford, Cambridge, Durham, London, Glasgow and Edinburgh, mainly to study medicine, law and engineering. The contacts of these overseas students were mainly with other students, faculty members, and landlords and landladies in the communities in the vicinities of the universities, and so their presence had little impact on the wider British population. After qualifying, students with contracts with their governments and those whose parents had funded their education returned to their countries of origin in the Caribbean where they practised their professions and were held in high esteem by the public. In time, some of them entered the political arena and were elected or appointed to positions of power and, eventually, some of them led their countries to independence. The returning professionals were regarded by the people in their countries as role models for their children, since education was considered to be the means for social, economic and political advancement.

World War II from 1939 to 1945 was the catalyst for large-scale immigration from the Caribbean to Britain. Seven thousand men enlisted in the Royal Air Force and according to Bonham-Carter (1987) were greeted by the Colonial Office with gratitude. Others were recruited to work as technicians in the various factories in the war industry, in the Forestry Commission or in munitions factories. Many worked in Merseyside, Manchester and Bolton until they were made redundant upon the return of ex-servicemen and the economic crisis of Britain of 1947.

Well-educated women, teachers and nurses eager to offer their skills to the war effort applied to join the Services. Whilst the men had been accepted readily, the British government, although in dire need of more personnel as the war dragged on, had reservations about admitting black women into the Women's Services. After much debate and negotiations between Britain and her powerful ally, the USA, women were reluctantly recruited in the latter days of the war to serve in the Auxiliary Territorial Service (Bousquet and Douglas 1991).

At the end of the war, some of the demobilized men and women chose to remain in Britain where employment chances were better, compared with the adverse economic situation in the Caribbean, and some grasped the opportunity to pursue further education. Others returned to their home countries only to find that there was a high rate of unemployment, and some of them responded to Britain's recruitment drive for labour and were eager to return to find work.

Large-scale post-war migration began when on June 1948 the SS Windrush docked at Tilbury docks with 492 passengers, the majority of whom were from Jamaica. The passengers were mainly men; some were ex-RAF servicemen, and others, who were employed, resigned their jobs in order to fulfil their ambitions of furthering their education through working and studying in Britain. There were teachers, artists, writers and other working class people from rural areas, all eager to work. Women were also among the passengers, many of them planning to train as nurses. By 1955, there were 13 ships making 40 sailings each year and several chartered air flights were arranged in order to bring men and women eager to work (Patterson 1965).

Most of the migrants regarded migrating to England as coming to the 'mother country'. This concept had far-reaching implications since they came from a region steeped in a culture of veneration for mothers and therefore felt it their duty to care for 'mother', now in difficulty. Some of the media were caught up in the euphoria of the time with the arrival of the Windrush and the *Evening Standard* of 21 June, 1948 proclaimed: 'Welcome home to the 400 sons of Empire.' The stark reality was that 'mother', represented by the British government, had not provided the provision to meet the basic needs of her children.

The indigenous British population knew little about the government's recruitment drive which was responsible for the influx of people from the Caribbean, and many expressed fears that their jobs would be taken away or that the newcomers intended to live freely on the welfare state. A notable factor which also influenced the migration from the Caribbean was American legislation, when with the passing of the McCarran Act (1952) the numbers of migrants entering the USA were limited. The restrictions were a severe blow to people from all over the Caribbean as formerly, the USA had been the most popular place for those seeking employment outside of the Caribbean region. The British recruitment drive was therefore timely for those eager to work who were denied the opportunity of migrating to the USA. The invitation also aroused their love for the 'mother country' who was in need of their help in a similar manner to the wartime call, when volunteers joined the armed forces to fight for king and country.

During the early days of the immigration it was not realized, or even accepted, that the people who arrived from the West Indies came from separate islands or the mainland territories of British Honduras (now Belize) and British Guiana (now Guyana), which comprised the British colonies in the Caribbean. Neither was it understood that in spite of similarity of skin colour, they were not a homogenous group. Hearing that the majority of the early immigrants arrived from Jamaica the indigenous people thought that all black people from the West Indies were Jamaicans. When individuals sought to correct this misunderstanding by giving the names of the islands from which they came, the information was either ignored or treated as of no importance. This dismissive attitude served to annoy individuals who valued their identity, born of a sense of belonging to a particular homeland, just as people from the four countries which comprise the UK value their birthplace.

Several writers such as Glass (1960), Davison (1962), Patterson (1965), Peach (1968) and Rose *et al.* (1969) have described the migration from the Caribbean to Britain and debated the push and pull factors which influenced it. Patterson (1965) argues that from the Caribbean there were push factors such as:

- over-population and under-development, resulting in chronic unemployment

- low wages

- a lack of economic diversity, opportunity and incentives

- a lack of opportunities for higher education and vocational training

- the West Indians' readiness to travel in search of a better economic life.

Patterson (1965) admitted that the adverse conditions in the Caribbean had existed for over half a century and consequently West Indians had travelled to find temporary or permanent employment in other countries, such as Panama and North, Central and South America, and she conceded that the major pull factor stimulating migration to Britain was full employment in a diversified and large-scale economy. This full employment was the result of the flight of white British workers from the less attractive and less well-paid jobs. Peach (1968) argued that the conditions in the Caribbean were improving at that time and that there was a demand for labour there. He observed that the volume of the migration followed the seasonal patterns of the British economy. He also suggested that there was a solid core of migrants who would have come no matter what the conditions, and another group which he called 'floating migrants' who would respond to reports of conditions.

The flow of immigrants was encouraged through direct recruitment of labourers. For example, the London Transport Executive, British Hotels, and the Restaurant Association recruited a substantial number of labourers directly from Barbados through the Barbadian Liaison Service (Rose *et al.* 1969). Some were also enticed to migrate through the recommendations of friends and fellow workers, but there were others who came not knowing where they were going to live, believing they would receive a welcome and be provided with basic amenities as they had come prepared to work to rebuild the country.

WOMEN AND CHILDREN

There were numbers of women among the early migrants, some accompanying their husbands with all or some of their children, and others also seeking employment or intending to join the nursing professions (as I have learned from conversations with some of these women).

It is estimated that during the peak period of the migration to Britain (1953–1956) 162,000 individuals migrated to Britain from the Caribbean, of whom 52 per cent were men, 40 per cent women and 8 per cent children. Between 1955 and 1960, adults brought 6500 children with them but left 90,000 behind in the Caribbean (Lowenthal 1972).

Many of the women who joined their husbands or partners left their young children in the care of grandmothers, who in some instances had been involved in the care of the children before their mothers left the country. Others relied on members of the extended family or friends. The mothers, like most of the migrants, had envisioned their stay in Britain to be temporary (approximately five years, which was the stated validity of passports), thinking that during that time they would be able to improve their financial status and would then return to live in less straitened circumstance in their countries.

Unfortunately for many of the immigrants their plans did not materialize, mainly due to low pay in the jobs available to them and the many unforeseen expenses, such as heating, purchase of warm clothing and travel expenses, which they had not envisaged. Some, disappointed and defeated by the poor standard of living and the blatant discrimination on the basis of their colour, returned home, but many were reluctant to do so without being able to demonstrate to family and friends that they had achieved their aims in migrating. Besides, there was no guarantee of employment in their home countries.

SERVICES FOR MIGRANTS

At the peak of the immigration in the 1950s, especially as such large numbers were coming from Jamaica, the Jamaican government seconded to Britain a Welfare Liaison Officer to assist them with problems common to newcomers in Britain. When more immigrants from other islands arrived, the British Caribbean Welfare Service took over the Jamaican civil servants' role in 1956. In 1958 when the British West Indian territories became a Federation, the service was extended and taken over by the Migrant Services Division of the Commission in the UK for the Caribbean, British Guiana (as Guyana then was) and British Honduras (Belize). One of the main duties of this service was to meet immigrants on arrival in Britain, having been informed by the authorities in the Caribbean of numbers, dates and places of arrivals.

The provision of these services was an indication that the West Indian governments sought to assist the immigrants in the early days of the immigration and were interested in their welfare. Davison, researching immigration from Jamaica in 1961, found that all those in the sample had been given addresses to which they could go on arrival in England (Davison 1962). Individual travellers or unorganized groups were not met and so it was difficult to know the exact numbers of immigrants or how to assist them if and when problems arose. As all British citizens from the British colonies had the right to travel to Britain there was no reason for the immigrants to be questioned about their whereabouts when they entered the country.

The migrants were relatively young with an average age of just over 30. According to the findings of a survey of Jamaican migrants (Roberts and Mills 1958), 75 per cent of men and women were in the 20–39 age group. They were eager to work and settled in about 40 towns and cities in England where the reviving industries were in need of labour. Large numbers settled in London, Birmingham, Manchester, Nottingham and Wolverhampton. Few of them went to Scotland or Northern Ireland.

Many of them lived in poor, over-crowded conditions which, according to Peach (1968), were:

> the product of housing shortages, prejudice and discrimination. There was general reluctance on the part of the white population either to sell or rent better accommodation to the West Indians so they were thrown back on making intensive use of any accommodation that was available to them. (Peach 1968, p.87)

Many of the first-generation migrants recalled their humiliating attempts to find housing and being refused because they were black. They were repelled by the notices on the houses of 'no dogs or Irish or coloureds', some of which also included 'no children'. When rooms were found in boarding houses, sometime one room was occupied by several persons with a shift arrangement for the occupancy of the bed on the proviso that each occupant was responsible for his or her bed clothes which were removed after use.

In time, the more enterprising bought old houses in need of extensive repairs and on short leases. As time went on and white residents moved out of the area, houses with long leases and freehold properties became available. They refused to be deterred from acquiring homes by the difficulties with banks refusing to give them mortgages. They reverted to a self-help scheme known in their countries as 'Partners' whereby a number of people agreed to subscribe an agreed sum, for a period of time such as a week, a fortnight or a month, with one person responsible for collecting and holding the money and paying it out as a lump sum until each had received their savings. The order of payment to each individual was agreed and the total would be paid to each person in turn, which would enable him to make the down payment on his house or other commodity. The advantage of this was the immediacy of obtaining a lump sump rather than waiting for individual savings to mount up. The payments continued until all members received the total of their payments. In this way individuals were enabled to amass the payment for their houses.

West Indians settled in areas where the white population was decreasing. In time the population of 'West Indians' increased both by a natural increase as the migrants were young and of child-bearing ages, and because of children entering the country to join their parents. Some home-owners rented furnished rooms to fellow migrants. This was described by a first-generation migrant, who expressed disappointment that the black landlord also exploited fellow migrants. The rents were high for the limited accommodation of a room with a paraffin heater, a cooker on the landing, a shared toilet and sometimes a bathroom. However, as more people bought houses in the areas where migrants lived, there was competition to attract tenants and so conditions of the houses and facilities were improved. When the borough councils in the cities housed the immigrants, they were usually placed in the poorest houses in old estates (Peach 1968).

RETURN OF MIGRANTS TO THE CARIBBEAN

One aspect of the movement of people from the Caribbean that is not often highlighted is that of emigrants who returned to their homes by 1959. Peach (1968) stated that when the Migrant Services was disbanded, the number of West Indians who returned to their countries of origin was among the statistics which were lost. Patterson (1965) expressed the view that some of the reasons for this return movement of migrants may have been the economic recession in Britain, and their apprehension and anxiety over the Nottingham and Notting Hill race riots of 1958.

Some may have succeeded in their aims of learning a skill, or acquiring enough money to purchase land or business in their own country, and there were those who were more comfortable living in their familiar environment. Some of those who stayed sent young children and infants back to their extended families. There were also those who requested repatriation because they had no industrial skills required in the available jobs, physical ill health, mental illness, illiteracy, or inability to adjust to urban life.

About 25 per cent of those who returned were women, some of whom were paid £30 for escorting young children who were being sent to extended family members because their parents were employed and caring for the children was difficult in the absence of nursery or child-minding services (Patterson 1965).

RESTRICTION OF IMMIGRATION

Under the British Nationality Act of 1948 all British subjects in the colonies were entitled to hold British passports and were free to enter Britain and settle, but the numbers of immigrants who entered during the mass migration up to 1960 met with the disapproval of some politicians who opposed it, and some members of the House of Commons made demands for control. There also emerged a panic about the 'black presence' which was conceived as a threat to the indigenous population. A Gallup Poll held in May 1961 showed that 73 per cent of the electorate favoured immigration control. Members of the Conservative Party at their conference in 1961 presented 39 resolutions in favour of control of immigrants. The Conservative government responded to the pressures about the numbers of immigrants and in 1961 introduced legislation in the form of the Commonwealth Immigrants Act which became effective on 1 July 1962.[2]

This action by the government seems to have encouraged the growing black and white racism culture; to be an immigrant was translated as 'black' and was linked with violence, crime and poverty. These perceptions of the immigrants by individuals and institutions who were blatantly racist undermined the self esteem of the migrants and aggravated their sense of separation and loss.

Peach (1968) expressed the view that it was clear from the debates held at the time that the purpose of the Commonwealth Immigrants Act was not to regulate the immigration, but to restrict the movement of people from predominantly 'coloured' countries. Before the Act was enforced, immigrants from the West Indies, especially dependants, hurried into Britain in an attempt to beat the ban, but the early months of the enforcement of the Act in 1962 coincided with a fall in demand for workers and so the inflow of migrants fell. It is interesting that by the end of the first year of the Act the statistics show that 468 West Indian men left Britain, and 3716 women and 3157 children arrived, and it may be assumed that they were not holders of vouchers. According to Peach, stricter scrutiny was then being applied to the family relationships of the dependants, to be certain that children between the ages of 16 and 18 were not being introduced as workers without vouchers. 'The imposition of strict controls was in harmony with public opinion' (Peach 1968, p.61).

Commenting on the significance of the Act, Bonham-Carter, who was the first Chairman of the Race Relations Board, and later of the Community Relations Commission, observed that there was a contradiction between the immigration policy which was intentionally discriminatory and the internal race relations policy which advocated equal treatment irrespective of race. 'This contradiction, so obvious to the minorities, struck at the roots of their confidence in the good intentions of the society they had joined' (Bonham-Carter 1987, p.2). I have often heard the training referred to as 'the race industry' by sceptics.

---

2   Under the Commonwealth Immigrants Act of 1962 persons wishing to work in the UK needed work vouchers. Category A vouchers were for applicants who had a job to come to in the UK, Category B were for applicants with skills or qualifications, and a limited number of vouchers were given to Category C, for those not included under Categories A or B. The vouchers were valid for six months and could be extended for a further six months if good reasons were shown (The Commonwealth Immigrants Act, Statistics 1963, Cmnd 2151, p.10).

The Act brought into being the first statutory body, the National Committee for Commonwealth Immigrants, which was given the mandate to promote the integration of the newcomers. Also, local voluntary organizations were funded by the central government. Formerly the voluntary organizations struggled from lack of resources and, above all, lack of knowledge or experience in handling the new situation caused by the influx of Caribbean migrants. Some men demobilized from the RAF and the army had settled after the end of the war, others had returned to their countries, but owing to lack of employment there had decided to return. They were active in voluntary organizations which not only helped and supported immigrants, but also served to provide advice to white workers in the field of community organization. Women, too, were engaged in community work and in the early work of race relations.

Two well-known African Caribbean figures who became involved in politics and race relations were the late Lord Learie Constantine and Dr David Pitt. Lord Learie Constantine was a well-known cricketer, who became a member of the Race Relations Board, a Governor of the BBC and was made a life peer in 1969.

Dr David Pitt, created a Baron in 1975, was a physician. He held many influential posts in London, for example Deputy Chairman of the National Committee for Commonwealth Immigrants, Deputy Chairman of Community Relations and Chairman of the Greater London Council. He was also a Founder and Chairman of the Campaign Against Racial Discrimination. There were several other notable men and women, indigenous people as well as those from the Indian sub-continent, who worked tirelessly in race relations in order to establish racial harmony and equality especially in the workplace. Peppard (1980) remarks that the younger generations of minority groups born in Britain are unaware of the vast efforts their predecessors made during the early years of immigration in order to promote the more equitable multiracial society in which they now live.

WOMEN MIGRANTS

The majority of women migrants had lived in the rural areas of their home country; they had only primary education and little or no training in skills applicable to the work in large-scale industries. Some of them had been self employed, sewing in their own homes, raising livestock and growing vegetables which they marketed, or were owners of small shops. They mostly lived in family units or if in their own houses these were in close proximity to family members and they were helped with child care and housekeeping by their mothers and members of the extended family, or friends. In the early days of the migration there were few extended family structures as obtained in the Caribbean, as generally grandmothers and older women had not migrated.

Patterson (1965) claimed that West Indian women migrants experienced more difficulty than the men. They had no experience of work in industrial units with industrial machinery and were unable to work fast enough to earn the basic wage. Some worked in small manufacturing firms and in laundries. Wages were low, and in some of the workplaces those who complained and tried to agitate for higher wages were dismissed. Since the women were young and of child-bearing ages, the pregnancy rate was high and some, in the absence of help, were unable to keep their jobs for any length of time. Some firms complained that when there was a group of women working together, they were inclined to be aggressive towards the local women. Patterson (1965), researching South London employment exchanges, found that few migrants were placed in clerical, professional or commercial occupations. In retail firms the jobs offered were as labourers or cleaners. Private employers in industry refused to offer clerical or staff jobs as the applications were usually of poor quality and there was the possibility of objections by their staff. It was also felt by the employers that the public would disapprove of being in close contact with black workers, but this supposition was never examined.

According to Patterson, in the years of full employment the management and members of staff tolerated the West Indian workers who were regarded as 'stop gap labour, slow, alien in habits and often difficult to deal with, a group that would be expendable in the event of recession' (Patterson 1965, pp.123–4).

In the 1960s many of the women who persisted in working in menial and low-paid jobs had the will to resist exploitation and, according to the narratives by some of these women, as related in the compelling book *The Heart of the Race* (Bryan, Dadzie and Scafe 1985), they started to confront employers and oppose the exploitation. They decided that they would refuse to accept the poor conditions, low wages, racism and sexist discrimination in the workplace. The trade unions were reluctant to support the women and often they were left to take on the employer individually. However, over the years, black workers were able to work collectively and by 1983 black women workers were recognized for their contribution towards the unions establishing caucuses which vigorously address racism and other issues which affect black workers in the workplace (Bryan *et al.* 1985).

The employment of large numbers of women in the National Health Service was the result of recruitment by the British government in the 1950s and the assistance through subsidies of governments of the countries in the Caribbean. In spite of the need of the service the migrants experienced difficulty, with many of them shunted into being auxillaries, or State Enrolled Nurses. Many of these were unable to continue to pursue the full training to become State Registered Nurses. For those who succeeded in becoming the latter, promotion was slow.

Many of the women who had joined the health service to become nurses never achieved their goals but were given domestic jobs within the hospitals. Black women were then at the bottom of the pile in the hospital hierarchy, but gradually when the economy began to decline white workers began to see the need for collaborative work.

WOMEN AND CHILD CARE

Women worked long hours and the opening hours of day nurseries were unsuitable, especially for mothers who had no one to collect the children and care for them until they arrived home. Many families shared housing which often left much to be desired in terms of privacy and comfort for themselves and their children. Some women accepted the services of unregistered child minders, while others sought the help of the social services and were offered places in residential nurseries. These had been established during the war and were mostly situated in the counties which were considered relatively safe from enemy bombing and to which children had been evacuated. At the end of the war, women were encouraged to return to their homes and to care for their children, thus the nurseries were under-used. It seems that whilst the social services perceived this to be a solution for the problem of the immigrant working mothers, the long-term consequences of the separation of young children from their mothers had not been considered. The immigrant population lived in the urban areas, their wages were low, they were unfamiliar with travel to the areas in which the nurseries were situated so visiting was infrequent and the children became attached to their carers. The staff of the nurseries were all white and since there was no contact with black people, the children were alarmed and fearful of their black mothers who were strangers to them.

The mothers stated that the staff dissuaded them from visiting as the children showed fear and were unsettled. Perhaps because the superiority of white people was generally accepted, and because they felt rejected by their children, the less assertive mothers accepted the advice and stayed away so that they did not upset their children whom they planned to take home when they were older.

Writing about 'West Indian' women living in London, Fitzherbert (1967) observed that mothers visited their babies in residential nurseries infrequently. She attributed the reason for the mothers' discontinuation of visiting to the 'West Indian' pragmatic attitude to life and stated that the child out of sight could very easily be out of mind and the longer children stayed in the nurseries, the more reluctant the mothers were to be reunited with them. This reluctance to reunite with children from whom mothers had been separated was not peculiar to West Indian mothers; English mothers were observed to exhibit similar reactions when in similar circumstances.

In a study of ten English mothers whose young children had been taken into residential care for periods ranging from six days to five months, Westheimer (1970) observed that five (50%) of the mothers whose children stayed for the longer period were reluctant to have them back and made various excuses why the reunion could not be effected. Westheimer did not criticise the English mothers for having a pragmatic attitude to the care of their children, even when she conceded that some of the mothers considered their wishes to the exclusion of the needs of their children. She argued that the mothers had stopped visiting 'as though to avoid seeing and feeling, and not to renew feelings of pain and guilt over loss of the child' (Westheimer 1970, p.3). Is it not possible that the West Indian mothers had similar feelings? Fitzherbert, in expressing the opinion that with the migrant mothers the children, once out of sight, could easily be out of mind, failed to consider that the guilt of leaving the children to be cared for by total strangers might have served to keep the children uppermost in their minds. Fitzherbert's conclusion seems to be a glaring example of the reluctance to recognize that there are similarities of feeling and reactions to separations faced by human beings regardless of racial or cultural backgrounds.

Many African Caribbean women refuted Fitzherbert's accusation and insisted that they thought about their children continually and bemoaned the fact that they were unable to care for them during the early years of their lives. No information was found about these mothers and children who suffered separation for long periods as a result of the children's stay in the residential nurseries: whether they were ever reunited and what the nature of their relationships with each other was, and how many of the children were cared for in children's homes that existed at the time.

Some mothers with young children decided to give up their jobs, acquired sewing machines and worked at home for garment manufacturers, even though this meant a decrease in earnings. Others who lived in nuclear families arranged matters so that they and their husband worked on shifts and were able to share the care of their children.

It was unlikely that the women had been given family planning advice in their own countries before they migrated since the service had not been introduced at the time; therefore in the early days of the migration, families tended to be large. Hood *et al.* (1970) found that the families they researched consisted of a mean of 2.5 children as compared with that of 2.3 for their indigenous neighbours. This had implications for the economic situation of the families since they were more likely than not employed in low-paid jobs. The emotional states of the mothers were difficult to assess but many of them seemed depressed and this had marked effects on their children who seemed to mirror the moods of their mothers.

MIGRANT CHILDREN AND SCHOOL EXPERIENCES

There were those who immigrated as nuclear families, anticipating that their children would be well educated in the English school system which was perceived to be exemplary. Some children were able to adjust to the schools which were less formal, than those in the Caribbean countries from which they came and settled. In the Caribbean, children were expected to be well behaved in classes and obedient to teachers. The teachers were strict in their discipline, and corporal punishment was administered for misdemeanours. Children respected the authority of teachers. However, they were discriminated against by peers and teachers, often being called racist names. In her autobiographical book *Coming to England* (1998), Baroness Floella Benjamin, who came to Britain to join her parents and other siblings at the age of 12, recalled the racist names, the rejection and taunting by peers. Theirs was a close knit family which communicated with each other and she and her siblings were advised that they should make sure to take advantage of all that was being offered in the way of knowledge.

Unfortunately others were disoriented in the schools and withdrew, and this was often interpreted as a sign of retardation. In their compelling book *The Heart of the Race*, Bryan, Dadzie and Scafe expressed the view that the attitudes of the teachers did the most lasting damage: 'Their concept of us as simple-minded, happy folk, lacking in sophistication or sensitivity became readily accepted' (Bryan *et al.* 1985, p.64). As a result of these attitudes of some teachers and educational psychologists, a number of children were labelled 'educationally subnormal' and placed in special schools (Coard 1971). Many of the parents were unaware of the consequences of the 'special school', thinking it was beneficial to their children. They did not know that they would be stigmatized and would find difficulty in being reinstated in mainstream schools. In some schools, children were assigned to doing chores outside of the classroom; if they showed an ability in sport this was encouraged to the detriment of their gaining educational skills. (However, in contemporary society some athletes have risen to the top of their chosen sport and represent the country internationally.)

HEALTH ISSUE OF MIGRANTS

Some of the women migrants suffered from mental disorder or mental illness and this was reflected in the number of admissions to psychiatric hospitals in the absence of counselling or therapy. There were various debates and much has been written about the 'misdiagnosis' of mental illness of African Caribbean migrants. Littlewood (1993) claimed that the speech of some of the women, which seemed to be unintelligible and a symptom of insanity to professionals, could be seen as a human response to disadvantage and racism.

I have always been concerned that some older migrants, in stressful situations, might unconsciously have used the language spoken in childhood which may have been the patois of another European language (for example, Spanish or French, the languages of some ancestors before the islands were colonized by the English as explained in Chapter 1), and this may have been assessed as unintelligible speech by professionals unaware of the cultural backgrounds of the clients and not recognizing the dialect. This could have led to faulty diagnoses and the individuals being admitted to hospital.

Within the black population, the rate of admission to psychiatric hospitals as involuntary patients under the Mental Health Act in the 1960s was two to three times higher than for the rest of the population. There was some evidence of higher dosages of drugs and, often, physical treatments such as electro-convulsive therapy were more frequently given, independent of the actual diagnosis (Littlewood 1986).

RELIGION

The migrants came from societies where the established churches were important to them, not only from the religious point of view, but also because they served as an agent of socialization. When they arrived in Britain, they were disappointed that the Church was not as vibrant as they had expected; also many of the churches were not welcoming. Some priests claimed that their congregations would prefer that the migrants did not come to their church. Some of the migrants established their own non-conformist churches where they felt a sense of belonging. Hill (1963), who had worked in Jamaica and among the migrant workers in London, deplored the establishment of all black churches, seeing them as a hindrance to integration, which the Church according to its gospel message was dedicated to preach and to promote.

This point of view was debatable as the elimination of religious difference was not a precondition of full citizenship. It was not exacted from other minority ethnic groups, so why was it thought to be necessary for the Caribbean migrants?

CONCLUSION

African Caribbean people migrated to Britain anticipating acceptance in the country which, throughout their lives in the Caribbean, had been regarded as the 'mother country', a metaphor accepted during the period of colonization. Some of the narratives of the first-generation immigrants provide vivid descriptions of the adversity they experienced, but they were prepared to work to achieve their aim of a better economic life. Regardless of their level of education and training received in the Caribbean, they were mostly assigned to manual jobs. They worked long hours, and often the wages were meagre and well below that of indigenous workers. Racism was blatant with name calling, refusal of employment or when employed denial of promotion; what was most distressing for most of the mothers was the absence of extended family members to assist them in caring for their young children and therefore the necessity to leave them in the care of strangers.

There were two marked differences for some of the migrants: namely, they lived in isolated nuclear families in urban areas, and in the absence of extended families, some of the husbands assisted in caring for the young children. These were remarkable shifts from the conditions under which most of them had lived, either in rural areas where families, relatives and friends provided social contacts and camaraderie, or in 'yards' (i.e. communal areas) in the towns in their home countries. First-generation migrants, having experienced the pain of separation from their home countries, yearned to return. Some invested in procuring land or building houses 'back home' and considered return home as most desirable when their children completed their education. This is another experience of broken attachments, separation and loss in the families when their children elected to remain in Britain. So the circle continues, probably until those born in this country feel a sense of belonging to the country of their birth.

The next chapter gives a brief description of attachment theory, the theoretical framework for the studies of the families.

Chapter 3

Attachment, Separation and Loss

A Brief Account of Attachment Theory

> Whilst especially evident during early childhood, attachment
> behaviour is held to characterize human beings from the cradle
> to the grave. (Bowlby 1979, p.129)

A great deal has been written about families of African Caribbean
origins; studies have been anthropological and sociological with mainly
structural and functional perspectives. When the migration from the
Caribbean to Britain began, and up until recently, there was a dearth of
studies which examined the psychological effects of the phenomenon
of the sharing of child-rearing and of child-shifting among extended
family members or others external to the family network either in the
Caribbean, or reconstituted families in Britain.

One reference found was that of Norris (1962) writing on Jamaican
family life. She claimed that children did not rely on the protection of
one set of parents; they learnt at an early age to distribute their affection
among the many mother and father substitutes within the extended
family. Whilst this may appear to be so, when multiple mothering is
closely observed, it is seen that children relate differently to persons in
the family and invariably seek out the primary carer, especially when ill,
hurt and in need of comfort.

In recent times in the Caribbean, studies of parent–child socialization
and the effects of unstable home environments are emerging. In Jamaica,
a study considering the living arrangements of children in whom
conduct disorder was prevalent found that a high percentage of them

had experienced changes two to six times in their parental living arrangements. It was suggested that the frequent changes in living arrangements may have affected the quality of attachment relationships with their parents (Crawford-Brown 1997).

In Trinidad and Tobago, a child psychiatrist drew attention to mental health issues and family socialization in the West Indies: 'mental health issues tied to attachment, separation and loss (see Bowlby 1973) are central to much of the psychopathology that may be specifics of Caribbean socialization' (Sharpe 1997, p.266). She further expressed the view that many children who experienced serial losses of carers to whom they were attached, having been shifted from home to home, are vulnerable to depression and sadness, aggressive impulses and low self esteem. However, other factors such as the child's age, gender, temperament and personality structure, and other socializing agents within the environment will affect clinical manifestations.

Here in Britain during the early days of immigration from the Caribbean, there were some teachers and social workers who were aware of the trauma of loss experienced by some children who, after varying lengths of time, had left their extended families to join their parents and new families. In one area of London, when children reacted in school with conduct disorders, they were referred to a Child Guidance Clinic. Mothers and children were diagnosed as suffering from depression which seemed to be a reaction to separation from their homelands and significant carers (Stewart-Prince 1968). Some of the mothers were referred to Nurture Groups and in these were able to express their feelings about missing their own mothers and their inability to react with warmth to the reunited children (Gorell Barnes 1977).

These feelings suggested that the women were feeling the loss of a primary attachment figure and demonstrated that reactions to broken attachments are also experienced by adults, as expressed in the quotation at the beginning of this chapter.

As stated in the introduction to this book, the theoretical base of the research on reconstituted families is attachment theory. In this chapter I shall briefly outline the theory and demonstrate its relevance to the studies of African Caribbean families who experienced broken attachments, separation and loss through the process of immigration from the Caribbean to Britain.

I consider it important to place the founder, John Bowlby, in the context of his family, his work and his research, in order to give the picture of how he arrived at producing his seminal work on attachment theory, separation and loss. A brief explanation of the work of his co-worker Mary Ainsworth will also be included.

John Bowlby was born in 1907, one of six children, and was cared for by a nursemaid as was the custom followed by upper-class families; she became his principal attachment figure during the early years of his life. When he was four years old she left the family. Richard Bowlby, son of John Bowlby, claims that the origin of his father's motivation to delve into parent–child attachment relationships probably stemmed from this traumatic event, and he writes from his father's reflection of the experience that he recalled that he was sufficiently hurt to feel the pain of childhood separation but was not so traumatized that he could not face working with it on a daily basis (Bowlby 2004).

There were several other experiences in his life which influenced his passion for finding a theory which would be of profound importance when applied in caring for young children, and especially useful in helping them to deal with traumatic losses of significant persons with whom they had formed an attachment.

Bowlby's biographers, Holmes (1993) and Van Dijken (1998), give accounts of some of these experiences. They include, during his early childhood, the absence of his father who was abroad during the war years; unhappiness at his first boarding school; the sudden death of his godfather and the silence in the family about the event, which may not have assisted him in coping with bereavement; his experience of teaching and relating with children considered to be 'maladjusted'; and his experiences with evacuated children during the war and homeless children cared for in institutions after World War II.

Whilst in his third year as a medical student Bowlby was attracted to the area of study which became known as developmental psychology. He left his clinical studies for a while to teach in a 'progressive school for maladjusted children'. He communicated with children whose behaviour was disturbed and disturbing, and he observed the seeming correlation between their difficulties and their unhappy and disrupted childhoods (Holmes 1993).

Early work at the London Child Guidance Clinic provided him with the opportunity to observe children and to develop his ideas alongside analytically oriented social workers. In the setting of the clinic, he was able to consider the transmission of neurosis across the generations. He saw that problems unresolved in the parents' childhoods influenced their reactions to their children, often adversely. Unlike Freud, who mainly worked with adults and associated their problems with some childhood trauma, Bowlby examined and treated children who presented with neurotic symptoms and disturbed behaviour. He explained that by working backwards into children's histories, he unearthed the common factor of deprivation of maternal care caused either by the children living in institutions or by being posted 'like parcels from one mother figure to another' (Bowlby 1952, p.32). Unfortunately his study was not validated by the examination of a control group of children who may have been subjected to similar experiences but who seemed unscathed.

Bowlby realized that his interests and views were not acceptable to the members of the British Analytical Society and he broke his relationship with the society and concentrated on his work observing closely the effects of maternal deprivation on the young child. In his early work during the 1930s and 1940s Bowlby wrote extensively on the psychological disorders of young children and expressed the view that unsatisfactory early experiences such as poor mother–child relationships or violence in the family could have contributed to them. He paid great attention to significant experiences of loss which might have occurred through separation from the mother or mother substitute during the child's early years, or through the death of a close member of the family. He was supervised for a while by Melanie Klein, but his views conflicted with hers in respect to the scant attention she paid to the importance of the environment on children's disturbed behaviour (Klein 1975).

Bowlby studied the case records of 44 juvenile thieves, collected between 1936 and 1939, comparing them with a control group similar in age and gender, who, although emotionally disturbed, did not steal. The aim of the research was to clinically demonstrate his convictions 'that separation of the young child from his or her mother or mother substitute was inherently traumatic' (Riley 1983, p.97).

Seventeen of the 44 children had been separated completely from their mothers or foster mothers for periods of six months or longer during the first five years of their lives. Only two from the control group had had a similar experience. Fourteen of the 44 'thieves' were described as affectionless characters, lacking shame and sense of responsibility, and having an inability to show affection. In the control group there were none to whom this description could be applied.

Bowlby considered that the high incidence of separation from their mothers among the affectionless thieves was highly significant and that it 'was an unusually clear example of the distorting influence of a bad early environment upon the development of personality' (Bowlby 1944, p.39). He also expressed the opinion that early separation adversely affected the ability to form and maintain relationships. He recommended that long separations of children at an early age should be avoided because of the serious damage which the separation had on the development of their characters, and he expressed his belief that if these separations were avoided, many of the cases of chronic delinquency could be prevented (Bowlby 1944). The controversy and discussion of the research was influential in drawing attention to the possible consequences of maternal deprivation on the developing child.

During the 1940s there was a shift from earlier harsh approaches towards children and according to Richardson (1993, p.39) 'an emphasis was placed on the importance of mother love for the normal, natural development of the child'. Gradually mothers and professionals changed their attitudes towards children. The increased interest in the field of developmental psychology influenced a growth of interest not only in physical development, but in psychological and emotional development as well. Nevertheless, during World War II young children were separated from their families through evacuation to avoid the dangers of the bombing of the cities. Convinced of the potential damage to children's personality development by prolonged separation, Bowlby and other colleagues, one of whom was Winnicott, advised the government against the evacuation of young children, but his concerns were not heeded. He believed that it was difficult for young children to understand why they had been sent away by their parents (Bowlby 1940). He recommended that children between the ages of two and five years should wherever possible be evacuated with their mothers as he believed in the importance of relationships in the early years of the life of the individual.

After World War II, Bowlby was commissioned by the World Health Organization to study the effect on institutional care of children deprived of normal home lives. In the report to the Organization on the mental health aspect of homeless children who had been reared away from their parents, he stated his belief that maternal care in infancy and in the early years of the child was essential. He expressed the necessity for the relationship of the child with the mother or mother substitute to be 'warm, intimate, continuous' and to be satisfying and enjoyable for both of them (Bowlby 1952, p.11). Yet again Bowlby was severely criticized for his emphasis on the mother caring for the infant, even though he spoke of 'mother or permanent mother substitute'. From his personal experience he would have known that it was possible for a mother substitute to establish a relationship as he described.

Among other statements about the ill effects of maternal deprivation in infancy he stated that there were long-term effects on intellectual and personality development even though children appeared to have recovered from months of deprivation. If the deprivation extended beyond 11 or 12 months of age, speech and other social abilities were likely to be affected.

Bowlby himself acknowledged the need for more research in order to justify some of his conclusions, such as whether there was a sensitive period of development when children were more vulnerable to maternal deprivation and the reversibility of impairment caused. Nevertheless, he believed that there was evidence which indicated that an infant between the ages of 7 months and 10 or 11 months was most vulnerable to the deprivation of bonds which had been formed with the primary carer.

In his criticism of Bowlby's report, Michael Rutter advanced the opinion that there were several types of deprivation during separation, besides maternal. Whilst we would agree with Rutter that children bond with fathers, siblings and other members of the family, it is observed that most children express a preference for their mother when they are stressed, or ill and wanting comfort. Rutter (1981) conceded that the concept of maternal deprivation was useful in drawing attention to the adverse consequences of inadequate care in the early lives of children. He also claimed that Bowlby's writings from 1961 to 1969 were most influential in discussions on mothering, but he observed that Bowlby's writings had often been misinterpreted and wrongly used to advocate 24-hour care by mothers.

Bowlby's work in developing attachment theory was helped considerably by Mary Ainsworth, an American, who had accompanied her husband on a work assignment in England, and obtained employment at the Tavistock Clinic as a research assistant to Bowlby during the 1950s. She had written a doctoral thesis on 'An evaluation of the concept of security' (Salter 1940) at the University of Toronto and in her thesis she had examined the degree to which the individual was secure or insecure and had devised a system for classifying levels of difference in interdependent relationships, so she was already interested in the nature of Bowlby's work. Following this, on moving to Uganda, she researched the extent and the nature of children's attachment to their mothers by observing their behaviour when separated and subsequently reunited with the mother, first among Ganda mothers and children in their homes in Uganda, and afterwards in homes and in laboratory situations in Baltimore, USA. In the studies, Ainsworth identified that when children engaged in exploration of their environment, their mother was used as a secure base to which they returned.

The latter research (Ainsworth *et al.* 1978) became known as the 'Strange Situation'. It was designed to assess the organization of attachment behaviour of 12-month-old infants when separated from and reunited with their mothers. To give a brief summary, the experiment lasted for 20 minutes, divided into three-minute periods, in which mother and child are in a room supplied with toys. At first they are alone, then a stranger joins them. The mother leaves the child with the stranger, returns; and then she and the stranger leave the child alone, and subsequently return. As the stress of the procedure accumulates, the observer is able to record the child's reactions to his or her mother's return, the willingness of the child to be comforted by the mother and the use of the mother as a secure base from which exploration could be continued. The procedure is described in Chapter 3 of *Attachment and Loss: Volume II* (Bowlby 1973).

Three patterns of responses were observed and classified as follows:

- A. Insecure/avoidant: The child showed little or no distress when the mother left the room and avoided her when she returned. Play was less spontaneous and the mother was watched warily.

- B. Secure attachment: The child showed some distress by crying and attempting to follow the mother, but responded to the stranger in the room and continued to play. The child showed pleasure on the mother's return and went to her to be comforted and quickly returned to play.

- C. Insecure/resistant/ambivalent: The child was very distressed when separated. When reunited with the mother the behaviour varied between accepting comfort from her and disengaging, between crying angrily and playing spasmodically.

In the experiment about 55–65 per cent exhibited type B pattern (secure attachment), 20–30 per cent type A (avoidant) and 5–15 per cent type C (ambivalent).

Following this experiment, other researchers continued to observe separation and reunion of mothers and infants of differing ages and gender, and at a later date a fourth pattern, D, was described and named 'Disorganized/disoriented' (Main and Weston 1982; Main and Solomon

1990). These researchers observed that 15–25 per cent of infants followed their mother to the door and screamed when she left the room. An attempt was made to greet the mother when she returned to the room, but then the infant turned away, sometimes lying face down on the floor seeming to freeze. Main and Hesse (1990) claimed that the child's disorganized behaviour occurred if the parent has been perceived as frightening or frightened. A number of children maltreated by parents, about 80 per cent, are found in this type D category (Main and Solomon 1990).

Crittenden (1985) also observed that this pattern of behaviour occurred when infants had been physically abused or neglected by the parent or when mothers suffering from mental disorder such as bipolar disorder were inconsistent and unpredictable in their treatment of their children. Mothers may themselves have suffered abuse in early childhood or they may have been grieving over the loss of a significant member of the family and have been unable to react emotionally to their children.

Bowlby (1973) claimed that when Ainsworth tested infants, first at 50 weeks and then again two weeks later, the babies showed increased distress during the mothers' absence on the second testing. This provided evidence that at one year old a brief separation in a 'bland situation' (unstimulating environment) can raise the sensitivity of a child to a repetition of the experience.

ETHOLOGICAL INFLUENCES

Bowlby stated that distress was observed in many species of mammals when the young became separated from a mother figure, and he noted how intensely the young clung to the mother figure when they were reunited. He was especially influenced by the work of Harlow in the USA with rhesus monkeys separated from their biological mothers. The monkeys were placed with surrogate mothers, one made of wire and one of cloth, and the behaviour of the monkeys was observed. The infant monkeys obtained their food from a bottle attached to the wire mothers, but spent most of the time clinging to the cloth mothers as they would have done with their real mothers and sought comfort and protection from them when frightened. Observation of these monkeys across the life span revealed that they experienced difficulty in relating to their peers and did not engage in the normal activities of young monkeys. When they matured, the males were often unsuccessful in mating and the females who reproduced refused to suckle their young and were inclined to be rough and punitive towards them (Harlow and Zimmerman 1959). Harlow concluded that the factor which seemed crucial to the difference in behaviour of the normal monkeys and the experimental monkeys was the presence or absence of a live mother. Bowlby considered this finding important in providing clues (even though animals cannot be equated with human beings) to the concept of attachment and attachment behaviour in humans.

Studies by Hinde (1965) in Britain complemented those of Harlow, and these studies helped to lessen the criticisms of the hypotheses of Bowlby and Ainsworth regarding the ill effects of deprivation of maternal care on the infant.

Bowlby's thinking was also influenced by Konrad Lorenz (1951), an ethologist who, investigating the instinctive behaviour of goslings immediately after being hatched, discovered that they followed him as they would their mother if she were present. This behaviour was called imprinting and once established did not alter. Lorenz attributed this behaviour to the goslings' need to maintain proximity to a seemingly protective figure during a sensitive period of life and not for feeding as goslings were perfectly able to find food. Bowlby utilized this concept and argued that whilst the human infant was unable to follow the mother or mother-substitute, he or she employed other means such as reaching out, crying, following with the eyes or smiling, in order to maintain contact. The responsive behaviour on the part of the mother or substitute was essential to the formation of secure attachment.

Observing that geese demonstrated bonding without feeding and rhesus monkeys fed without bonding, Bowlby argued that an attachment system was unrelated to feeding (Holmes 1993). The work of ethologists (for example, Barrett 2006) confirmed Bowlby's conviction that the primary need of children was for 'continuous, stable and responsive care', and that humans share with animals the need for security, which has a crucial biological function.

Bowlby (1982b) refuted the claim made by some clinicians – of whom Brody (1981) was one – that attachment theory was another version of behaviourism. He thought that the claim was based on scant knowledge of his work set out in the third volume of *Attachment and Loss* (1980) and attributed the misperception partly to his failure to draw the distinction between attachment and attachment behaviour. He gave the following definitions:

> *Attachment* is a strong disposition of a child or older person to seek contact with and to be near someone perceived to be reliable, especially under conditions of discomfort, illness or fear.
>
> *Attachment behaviour* is a biological function in which individuals engage in order to ensure protection. Human beings at various stages of the life cycle engage in various forms of behaviour in order to maintain proximity to a preferred person.
>
> (Bowlby 1982b, pp.668–9)

Bowlby later claimed that central to his concept of parenting was the secure base provided by both parents which allowed children and adolescents to explore the world outside of the family, confident that upon return there would be a warm welcome, they would be made comfortable, physically and emotionally, and if distressed would be listened to and comforted. In short, the parent would be available and responsive to the child when necessary without undue intervention (Bowlby 1988).

Bowlby held the view that if a young child experienced sensitive care in the early years from a co-operative and responsive mother, and later from a father, then that individual developed a sense of worth and was able to use the experience as a model for forming relationships in the future. He introduced the concept of children utilizing the memories of interpersonal experiences and, by so doing, developed the concept of Internal Working Models which influence expectations of how others are likely to behave towards the child and how the child will react towards others (Bowlby 1982a).

A child with a secure attachment tends to be more rewarding to care for and is usually a happier child than one whose attachment is insecure (either insecure/ambivalent, or insecure/avoidant). Sometimes the child with the latter pattern of attachment behaves as if he or she is confident and self reliant. This is usually a false presentation which masks fear or anxiety. However, it is possible to help parents in their parenting to recognize that the insecure child needs sensitive care and reassurance through love and affection. When the child is gradually experiencing the adults to be consistent and dependable, the pattern of behaviour begins to change (Bowlby 1988).

SEPARATION AND LOSS

Bowlby claimed that the 'loss of a loved person is one of the most intensely painful experiences any human can suffer' (Bowlby 1980, p.7). He believed that the cause of unhappiness, psychiatric illnesses and delinquency could be attributed to loss and believed that in working clinically with children and adults, this factor was often missed (Bowlby 1965).

Some of the work in Britain which informed Bowlby's research was the first recorded observations of the reactions of young children separated from their mothers and cared for in day nurseries during the latter part of World War II. Anna Freud in the Hampstead Nurseries observed a particularly turbulent reaction to parting from their mothers, with some children refusing to eat or sleep or be handled by strangers. Some had difficulty in recognizing their mothers when they visited but remembered their playthings which they had had before separation (Freud and Burlingham 1973).

James Robertson, a social worker who had witnessed grief reactions of the children in the Hampstead Nurseries and a member of Bowlby's research team, observed children who were hospitalized. The reactions of young children when separated from mothers were classified as 'Protest', 'Despair' and finally 'Detachment'. Often it seemed that there was misunderstanding of the stage of detachment and this was considered as the child coming to terms with the loss, whilst what occurred was the building up of a defence against feeling hurt again. Robertson made a film, *A Two-year-old Goes to Hospital* (1952), which showed the distress of the child when separated from her mother. This was not very well received, but another film, *Going into Hospital with Mother*, demonstrating the difference in the child's ability to cope with the physical illness, was well received. A further series of films made by Robertson and Robertson (1967–1972) demonstrated the adverse reactions of children separated from their mothers to whom they were attached, even when fathers visited them regularly in their foster home.

As a result of the films it was found that separations were not as traumatic if, for example, the children had been able to visit the hospital prior to being admitted, parents were allowed to visit regularly, children were allowed to take their favourite toy with them to hospital, and so on. The findings of Robertson's research and the films contributed to the changes made to the care of children in hospitals (see Ministry of Health 1959; Davies 2010).

Bowlby examined the sequence of reactions which children showed on being separated from their parents and from their mother specifically; he linked it to the pattern of mourning in adults who were bereaved and in this he refuted the common assumption that children were unable to mourn. He was further influenced by Marris (1991) who studied the responses of widows to the deaths of their husbands and observed that the reactions were similar to those of separated young children. The comparisons which Bowlby made between the responses of children separated from their mothers or parents and the mourning of adults were criticized, but over a period of time his views were vindicated and his conclusions were supported by, among others, Parkes, who also stressed that experiences of disruption of relationships and loss lasted through the life span (Parkes 1972). Bowlby's research led him to believe that trauma and loss are central in the case of neurosis, which is frequently based on unmourned loss.

Attachment theory has been studied extensively in the context of the mother and the young child. Bowlby's writings between 1969 and 1980 which produced the *Attachment and Loss* trilogy stimulated researchers to continue exploring the theory. Ainsworth's device of the 'Strange Situation' (Ainsworth and Wittig 1969), which focused specifically on the child's response to separation and reunion, has been extensively used with cross-cultural and intra-cultural variations and is regarded as a valid and reliable tool. Whilst the focus was on young children, others such as Main, Kaplan and Cassidy (1985) and Cassidy (1988) have observed attachment patterns in older children and adults. The attachment dynamic does not end in infancy but continues through life and is particularly activated in adults at times of distress (Holmes 1994). It seems therefore important to conduct contemporary investigations of the long-term meaning of maternal deprivation and disrupted attachments in adults who seem unable to make and sustain relationships.

RELEVANCE TO THE CARIBBEAN STUDY

Holmes (1998) observed that a central concept which has emerged from attachment theory is that of narrative, and he argues that a person's core state is a condensed form of his or her primary relationship. In attempting to study the long-term meaning of separation and reunion of the African Caribbean women, narrative was considered the most useful tool to help them to recall and reflect upon their experiences of attachment, separation and loss during their early lives.

It was ironic that, during the 1950s, mothers from the Caribbean were leaving their children behind to enter the labour market in Britain when Bowlby's theories about maternal deprivation, and about the traumatic effects of separation of young children from their primary carers, were being heatedly discussed especially by feminists and those who misquoted Bowlby as advocating 24-hour care by mothers. Bowlby made it clear that he never expressed such views (Bowlby 1982a).

In the Caribbean countries which the migrants left, having members of the extended family care for children was accepted as a cultural norm, just as in middle-class families in Britain nannies taking care of children was accepted. At that time there were no studies to investigate the emotional disadvantages children suffered through being shifted from one carer to another, and how their behaviour, their educational achievement or their ability to make social relationships were affected.

The early ages of the children who were left in the care of the extended family in the Caribbean and the long separations before reunion with mothers played a significant part in their inability to make satisfactory relationships in the reconstituted families. Some of the children who were left had been breast-fed by mothers up to the age of nine months and, according to attachment theory, after six months of age the child begins to demonstrate attachment behaviour towards the caring adult. If the adult is responsive, an attachment begins to be formed. This first attachment had been broken when the child was left with other carers, but many of the children had been left in a familiar environment with familiar grandparents and other members of the extended family, and they had become securely attached to their carers.

When the children were separated from their surrogate mothers they suffered the loss of all that was familiar to them but they were not given the opportunity to mourn. Those children who had not experienced contact with their mothers for long periods of time (the mean length of time in the sample was seven years) felt that they and their mothers were strangers and the behaviour patterns were mostly avoidant or resistant. The mothers' early experiences were important in how they were able to relate to their children. Some of them were unable to relate to the reunited children, who reacted with anger and resentment, and the emotional health of some suffered.

However, many of the children seemed to have had positive Internal Working Models from their secure relationships with their mother substitutes and were able to surmount many of the difficulties of the new environment, build new relationships with peers and have successful relationships with their families.

The early expressed views of Bowlby – that maternal deprivation affected the young child adversely – were severely criticized, and his writings on several aspects of the importance of early childhood experiences for development and behaviours in the later life of the individual were, and still are, misquoted. However, in progressing his research and formulating attachment theory he has provided a framework for psychological work not only with families and young children, but also with vulnerable clients in helping them to make and sustain relationships which help in living fuller lives.

The chapters which follow describe the experiences of the parents who left their small children for long periods before being reunited with them, and give the findings of a reflective study of adults who had been left as children and joined their parents in reconstituted families in Britain.

Chapter 4

Narratives of African Caribbean Mothers Separated from and Reunited with their Children

> The mothering of a child is not something which can be arranged by roster; it is a live human relationship which alters the characters of both partners… (Bowlby 1952, p.67)

When the mothers in the research study who had been separated from their children were reunited with them, relationships were far from satisfactory. These mothers became painfully aware that, as Bowlby (1952) emphasized, mothering is a live human relationship in which continuity is necessary.

This chapter is an account of interviews with 66 mothers aged between 32 and 50 years. My research study aimed to discover some of the factors which some migrant mothers perceived to be important in influencing the relationships between themselves and their children when reunited, after having been separated for relatively long periods of time.

The mothers were selected at random from attendance registers of classes in two secondary schools in south-east London and north-west London after conducting a pilot study of 20 mothers. They were divided into two groups. Thirty-eight were those separated from their children, who had been born in the Caribbean and left there when their mothers migrated, for periods varying from 1–13 years (a mean length of

6.2 years), mainly with grandmothers or maternal aunts. These were the Experimental Group (Group E). Group C consisted of 26 mothers whose children had been born either to them in England or had been born in the Caribbean and brought to England with their mothers at an early age; they had only been separated for a mean length of time of one week.

Eighty per cent of the sample were married and lived in nuclear families with 50 per cent in both groups occupying their own homes. There was a decided tendency to move away from multiple occupancy of houses which had been a necessity in the early years of the immigration (see Chapter 2). Remembering the early days of their lives in England, and the poor conditions under which they had lived, these families had resolved to provide homes as comfortable as possible for their families.

Those who lived in flats situated in large housing estates, owned by the boroughs and managed by the councils, deplored the drabness and the poor architectural design. For example, when it rained the balconies became flooded and it was difficult to enter the flat without being drenched. Nevertheless, as with most of those living in their own homes, they had decorated and furnished them tastefully. All of the homes contained television sets, with one family boasting of the possession of two sets, so that the children were able to watch their favourite programmes without interruption from the parents who did not always share their taste. The opportunity was therefore lost for children and parents to watch and discuss the contents of a programme. Little did parents foresee the possible dangers to their children of having television sets in their bedrooms without their knowledge, or control of the programmes, nor the amount of time spent viewing at night. Children were often deprived of sleep which caused them difficulty in staying awake during the day in their classes at school.

Most of the demographic characteristics of the two groups were similar. The differences occurred in the size of the family and age range of the children. In both groups the number of children born to mothers ranged from one to eight; however, the mothers in Group C tended to have smaller families – of the mothers who started their families in England only one gave birth to seven children, and the other mothers in that group with six, seven or eight children had given birth in the West Indies and brought their children to England. These mothers also stopped bearing children sooner than those in Group E. This may be attributed to the exposure to family planning information in Britain as most of them would have left the Caribbean islands before family planning programmes were initiated. Mrs Bailey, a mother of five children, three of whom were born prior to her arrival in England, said:

> 'Children just come: I didn't know about family planning. I think if more West Indians knew, they would not have them.'

Some of the mothers in Group E had been encouraged on arrival in Britain to use certain contraceptive devices, but a number of them were inclined to complain of discomfort and expressed some anxiety and worry about their continued use. There were no complaints from mothers in Group C and the size of their families more often conformed to the patterns of the indigenous population. These families desired and accepted smaller families, agreeing that it was impossible to maintain a high standard of living with large families in Britain.

In a study of one-year-old children of West Indian immigrants in Paddington, Hood *et al.* (1970) expressed surprise that 65 of the 101 mothers were legally married and seemed dubious that the marriages would stand the test of time. She advanced the opinion that 'it could be that the pattern of change has been effected too quickly, and adjustment will bring its crop of divorces or separations' (Hood *et al.* 1970, p.37). In both groups of the research sample in my study, their marriages had stood the test of time, with some of the couples married for periods of 15 years or more.

ATTITUDES TO PREGNANCY AND CARE OF BABIES

Most mothers claimed that at the time of the births of their children they were not very much concerned with the gender of the child. Two mothers had wished for girls, but the babies were boys and they were very disappointed at the time, but gradually came to terms with them being boys.

One mother in Group E said there was little interaction between herself and the baby besides breast-feeding. She was happy that her mother took full responsibility, so that she could continue her life as usual. One striking difference was that mothers in Group E, with children born in the Caribbean, were assisted with the care of their babies by their mothers whilst those of Group C, who started their families in Britain, relied on child-minders or on friends to assist them and a number of them cared for the children themselves.

The majority of the children of both groups were healthy babies and were easy to care for. Mothers breast-fed their babies, the mean duration of breast-feeding by mothers with children born in the Caribbean was 7.8 months; only 7 of the 38 mothers worked outside of the home. More than 50 per cent of the mothers in Group C worked full time and the mean duration of breast-feeding was 4.8 months by these mothers. They regretted that they were unable to do so for longer periods as they would have done in the Caribbean, but working full time necessitated the early weaning of the children.

It was interesting to observe that in reply to the question 'What did you do with your child when not looking after his or her physical needs?' 44 per cent of the 38 in Group E said they dressed them and took them out walking, but the grandmothers engaged in the talking and singing and playing with them; 20 (71%) of the 28 mothers in Group C said they talked and played with their children. Both these behaviours had implications for the development of attachment and the building of relationships between the carers and the children.

LENGTH OF SEPARATION FROM CHILDREN

Another difference between the mothers of the two groups was the pattern of separation from their children. Those in Group C experienced relatively brief separations from their children in the early years. Periods ranged from one week to one month, and these separations were due to mothers being in hospital for the birth of a second child. They admitted to being very worried over the fact that the children were left in the care of strangers, or with friends, who lived in housing unsuitable for the children's safety.

Twenty-two per cent of the mothers in both groups were unemployed and cared for their children themselves, whilst others who were either unable to obtain a nursery place or find a registered child-minder shared the caring with their husbands or partners. These fathers, who worked on evening shifts, cared for the children during the day whilst the mothers worked. For African Caribbean people, this was a new pattern of child care, where fathers were moving from being uninvolved with the rearing of the children to becoming the significant figure in the children's lives during their early years. This arrangement was advantageous in that the children were kept in their homes with a familiar figure with whom they were able to form an attachment, but there were some disadvantages.

Fathers who had worked long hours were often tired and besides looking after the physical needs of the children were unable to engage in play and activities vital for children's all-round development. Another disadvantage was that some mothers were unable to return home before the children were ready to be put to bed and there was not much time for mother–child interaction. Sometimes the children were kept up until late hours which often became problematic when they attained school age and did not get enough sleep; this was noticed in their lethargy at nursery school.

In Group E the separation from the children who had been left in the Caribbean continued for several years, with the mean length of time 6.2 years.

The bulk of unsatisfactory relationships occurred among the mothers and children in Group E.

AGE OF CHILDREN WHEN SEPARATED

In both groups most of the separated children were separated between birth and aged three years. The mothers in the study were insightful in seeing the age at which their children were left as an important factor in influencing the reunions with their children and whether these were satisfactory or unsatisfactory.

Twenty-two of the 38 (58%) mothers in Group E had left their children at the age of 0–3 years. They were unanimous in voicing the opinion that the young age at which they left the children had been crucial since, as one mother said, 'The one who cares for the child is the one he loves.'

Mrs Green left her son when he was one year old and they were reunited when he was ten years old. She said:

> 'It was a mistake to have left him when he was a baby, but I didn't know things would turn out so. He did not grow with me, his grandparents said they wanted him; I felt he belonged to them. Perhaps I don't really know him and he would not talk to me or to his father. He misses them at home as he grew with them and he doesn't feel myself and his father are his parents.'

Mrs Arthur's son was two years old when he was left with his grandmother and was reunited with his mother in Britain at five years; she related that he was used to calling his grandmother 'Mum' and called her by her first name. They did not communicate with each other and she considered him a disappointment, especially as he did not progress at school.

A single mother who had a satisfactory reunion with her daughter, whom she had left at five years old and with whom she was reunited when she was 15 years old, attributed the success of their relationship to her maintaining contact by writing letters to her when she started school so she knew her as her mother even though separated by distance. This mother summed up the separation and reunion problem of the migrants by saying that many mothers who had not communicated with the children during the period of separation tried to demand love from them when they arrived and expected them to conform to their way of doing things without realizing that the children did not know them. Since they were left when they were in their early stages of development they loved their caretakers.

As in the case of Mrs Arthur (above), some of the children growing up with their grandmothers had called them 'Mum' and heard their mothers being spoken of by their first names. It was more likely that they had conceptualized the persons being spoken of as siblings and so on meeting it was difficult to address mothers as 'Mum'.

Mrs Daley, who had a satisfactory relationship with her daughter who was left at four years old and reunited at age 14, related:

> 'She never called me anything. She would say "umm, ah", and when I said "Call me Mum or Mummy," she said "I left Mummy at home." I did not press her, we used to laugh about it and gradually she came around to calling me Mum.'

This mother described herself as easy-going and was not annoyed as she felt it was not the child's fault; she thought that her grandmother could have asked her to call her 'Granny' rather than 'Mum'.

Not being addressed by the traditional terms used for mothers seems to have been particularly distressing for those mothers who were more rigid about roles and status within the family. They could not tolerate their children calling them by their first names as they considered it disrespectful and did not consider that in growing up with grandmothers and extended family that would have been the name they had learned.

This reaction to not being called 'Mum' by the reunited child immediately when they arrived was similar to the findings of Burke

(1974), who researched mothers living in Birmingham. He concluded that it seemed that, psychologically, mothers needed to be called 'Mummy'. When there was reluctance on the part of the child to do so, it aroused anger in some mothers who became aggressive and withheld communication. Very probably the children didn't know the reason for their mothers' actions and became unloving and rebellious themselves as a result. In some instances, fathers took sides with the children, leaving mothers isolated and anxious and devoting their attention to the younger children in the family.

Most of the mothers in the sample felt deprived of their children. They understood that it was natural for the young child to become attached to the ones who had cared for them in their early lives, but the mothers' expectations were that as the children developed, they would show their appreciation for all that had been done for them, and would love and value them.

On reflection, the mothers who had brought older children with them regretted that they had not left the older children, who would already have formed a relationship with them in their early years and had a memory of them, and brought the younger ones. These mothers had worked hard to provide the necessities of life for the children by sending remittances to the carers in the Caribbean for clothes and toys and felt a sense of achievement in finally reuniting with the children. When the children arrived and did not even call them 'Mother' they realized that they were not as important to them as they had imagined themselves to be. Their pride was hurt and their self image badly shaken.

Bearing in mind that not all of the mothers who had left their children aged 0–3 years had unsatisfactory relationships, there must have been other factors that were of vital importance to the satisfactory or unsatisfactory reunions. Mothers cited length of separation as a factor.

This comment was made after mother and child were separated for six years:

> 'He stayed with his grandmother too long to really appreciate me as his mother. I wasn't happy at all; I felt I had committed a crime, making him think his grandmother was his mother.'

Another mother, reunited after separation for nine years, commented:

> 'You cannot have the love for these children, you cannot accept them as yours when they stay away so long. I just cannot get close to him, we are strangers. If only he had come earlier.'

The mothers with unsatisfactory relationships were distressed that, as the biological mother, they were unable to feel 'close' to their children, and the children were not close to them; in other words they did not have an attachment with each other. Mothers said they thought of the children constantly during the separation and the children out of sight were not out of their minds. They had protested at the separation. As one mother recalled, 'From the time I left I used to cry, and could not eat.'

They had despaired, as described by another:

> 'Oh, it was terrible. I would just stay like that and the tears would roll down my face even at work and I asked myself, "Why did I come? Is it worth it?"'

But they fought against detachment, even after other children had been born to them in Britain. They sought to foster attachment through sending parcels of clothes and money back home. Mrs King recalled:

> 'I would feel much better when I left the post office after posting that money. I would be so worried if there was any delay that prevented me from sending it.'

When the children arrived and they were unable to relate with love and affection as they had expected, the mothers realized that the material provision for the children had not been a sufficient substitute for being close to them and meeting their emotional needs during the early years.

One mother who had a positive relationship with her daughter who had been left at age five and had been reunited after three years, said:

> 'It was forever on my mind, I wanted her to come, I did not want to leave her too long. She grew with me and I stayed at home to look after her.'

This mother considered that making her child feel safe during the first years of being in the different and strange environment was essential.

MOTHERS' INTERACTION WITH CHILDREN PRIOR TO SEPARATION

The mothers in Group E were pleased that they had breast-fed their children as they thought 'mother's milk was the best'. Since the majority of the mothers did not work outside of the home breast-feeding had not posed a problem, as explained by Mrs Jones:

'I breast-fed him for eight months. I was at home and there was nothing else to do but look after him, if he cried I knew it was for something, so I saw to it that he was fed and dry.'

Another said:

'I breast-fed him for a year. I played with him, but if he cried and went on too long I would be worried. But my mother did most of the caring.'

Mrs Dean, who had lived in a nuclear family with her husband and child without the help of an extended family, prided herself on being a disciplinarian:

'I breast-fed him for seven months and gradually stopped as I was preparing to immigrate. I would walk him out in the afternoons, I would feed, bath and dress him and put him in his cot whilst I did the housework. I never paid too much attention when he cried as long as I knew he was well, and not hungry, as I believe children must learn from small, and I would leave him to cry himself to sleep.'

When he was nine months old her son was left in the care of his grandmother and his mother thought he was spoilt by her as she thought that she needed to compensate for the strict regime of his mother during the early months. Reunited when he was 14 years old, the reunion was unsatisfactory as the son missed his grandmother and his mother was very strict, trying hard to ensure that he did not go down a delinquent path in the strange society where he was unaware of the pitfalls.

The responses suggested that some mothers were concerned with meeting the physical needs of their children which they thought demonstrated their love, whilst grandmothers responded to the feeling and emotional needs of the children.

LEVEL OF CARE BY CARETAKERS

The majority of mothers trusted the grandmothers who were the main caretakers of the children and seem to have believed that grandmothers were able to rear their children who would grow up to be as adequate and capable as they (the mothers) felt themselves to be.

Those who related satisfactorily with the reunited children, especially the girls, claimed that grandmothers had been consistent in their discipline and that when the children joined them there was a similar pattern of parental behaviour. But some of the mothers who had unsatisfactory relationships with the reunited children thought that grandmothers had been permissive and indulgent with the children, especially if they were the first grandchildren and were boys.

Mrs Green gave voice to this:

> 'He was her first grandchild, and you know how these grandparents are with their grandsons. They allow them to do what they want to do. When our son came we had to be strict with him.'

This mother's statement indicated that she and the father agreed on the nature of the discipline they would employ. Nevertheless, the swing from an easy-going home to one with strict boundaries may have added to their son's anxiety and fear of the new family and environment and militated against a loving relationship.

Other mothers related that some of the caretakers, especially those who were not members of the extended families, were not caring and the children were neglected. They were treated as domestic servants and the remittances sent by parents were often appropriated and used to the advantage of their families. These mothers believed that the children must have thought they were abandoned by them and were therefore resentful and unloving towards them when they met.

YOUNGER CHILDREN IN THE RECONSTITUTED FAMILIES

Many of the mothers spoke about being pleased when other children were born to them in Britain, and spoke of them as having replaced those who had been 'lost' to them when left with extended families in the Caribbean. Mrs Dean recalled:

> 'I was very happy to have my son born here, as I was missing the ones I had left behind.'

Mrs Green said:

'This was like my first child for myself. I felt the older one belonged to my parents.'

Other mothers repeated similar feelings about the children born to them in Britain, and admitted having a closer relationship with the children from whom they had not separated. They thought that the reunited children, being chronologically older, did not need as much of their attention and demonstration of love and affection. It was a father who expressed the need to acknowledge the child's regression and the necessity to treat him with patience and loving care.

Some of the children who were older than toddler age, and had adequate language to talk with their carers about their mothers to whom they had become attached before separation, seemed to have retained interest in and affection for their mothers. Mothers were therefore able to relate to them more easily, introduce them to the younger children positively and so give them a sense of belonging to the new family. But there were instances when the younger children resented the presence of the reunited children in the home and mothers overlooked their behaviour, leaving the newcomers to think that the mothers loved the younger children more than them. This was an understandable observation on the part of the children as mothers had not been attached to the reunited children, so were closer to the children from whom they had never separated.

THE CHILDREN'S PROGRESS AT SCHOOL

Among the reasons for parents immigrating to Britain was the desire to provide the opportunity for their children to obtain better education, and to have the satisfaction of seeing them achieve what they had not. All of the mothers were ambitious for their children and those whose children were bright and progressing well in school experienced a sense of achievement. In every instance of unsatisfactory relationships with their children, mothers voiced their dissatisfaction with their children's educational attainment. Some of the mothers were critical of the school system and suspected that the children were not encouraged to learn and to aim at professional careers. They interpreted this as another instance of racial discrimination, and an attempt to prevent black people from moving from their lower socio-economic status.

Mrs Blake gave the following example:

'My son was bright and interested at school and his ambition was to become a doctor. He was sitting for his O levels. When he saw the careers officer and told him that he wanted to be a doctor, he was given a form to fill for a nurse's auxiliary. I refused to sign the form.'

Some mothers were not as assertive and felt unable to challenge the 'authorities'. Some likened the attitudes of some of the teachers to that of slave-owners bent on keeping black people in the lower class of society.

Many of the mothers were relieved when Saturday Schools were established in the late 1960s in order to provide supplementary education for their children. Saturday Schools are still considered necessary, decades later, as many African Caribbean parents still perceive the education system as impacting negatively on their children (Goring 2004).

GENDER OF THE CHILDREN

There was a tendency for mothers to relate more satisfactorily to girls than to boys. Some of the factors which contributed to this trend could have been the following.

It may have been that the discipline imposed upon the mothers when they were children was similarly imposed by the grandmothers upon the girls and the insistence upon assisting with household tasks was not new for most of the girls when they joined their mothers. The girls therefore fitted into the routine of family life more easily.

When boys joined the family, especially if they were the oldest in the family, some mothers delegated household tasks to them. Having not been in the habit of doing these tasks which were done by women and girls in the Caribbean, they were not competent in doing them and were often resentful at being expected to do them. Besides, they quickly learnt that their peers of the indigenous population did not do household duties.

It was significant that when mothers considered their relationship with boys as satisfactory, they frequently remarked that the boys were helpful in the house.

RELATIONSHIPS WITH HUSBANDS

Most of the women in both groups claimed that their relationships with husbands were satisfactory, as they were their main supports in the absence of extended families.

Mothers appreciated the co-operation and assistance which the husbands gave in the care of the children, the communication between themselves and also the communication between fathers and children. Where they were stepfathers to the reunited children, mothers were pleased that the children were accepted and were not a cause for embarrassment and discomfort in the home. (The relationship with fathers will be discussed further in the next chapter.)

A single mother who considered that she had successfully reared her son said:

> 'Although I missed the support of a partner, it is better for me and my child to live without a husband or partner than with one who did not treat us properly.'

FEELINGS ABOUT THE NEW ENVIRONMENT

Some of the women who came to England without their children and with only their husbands had no close friends or relatives. Most husbands worked long hours and there were hardly any opportunities to engage in social activities. Life was unstimulating, so many sought work as much to relieve the boredom as to improve their economic status. 'It was from home to work and back' said one woman. Some watched programmes on the television, but they missed contact with friends and were not sufficiently confident to go out alone.

Mothers voiced the feeling of discomfort of finding themselves the minority among the majority white population. Mrs Green remarked:

> 'We are not used to many things, the city life, the Social Welfare, the freedom the children have; but if there wasn't the prejudice, and the people here would accept you and teach you the way of their country it would be better. Even now we are not sure of the English people and what they really mean, and we are not sure of ourselves. Until this prejudice is completely gone, we are not sure.'

Government made attempts to eliminate racial discrimination through introducing various anti-discrimination laws, before finally passing the Race Relations Act (1976) but whilst the law was, and still is, to some extent, instrumental in minimizing discriminatory behaviour, it is difficult to legislate against attitudes. Unfortunately there is still evidence of racist behaviour at individual and institutional level which is disadvantageous to some African Caribbean people at all levels in the society.

Some mothers spoke of their fear for their children in society. They believed them to be at risk from white groups or from the police and in many instances this fear was justified. One mother described the environment as 'a jungle out there, with the lions waiting to devour them'.

Many of the mothers expressed the opinion that very often black youths were made the scapegoats and were wrongly accused of crimes and unjustly treated by the police. In some incidents where African Caribbean youths were the victims at the hands of white attackers, the police failed to pursue the incidents diligently and there was often no conviction of the perpetrators. Over the years there have been several incidents which confirmed some of the fears of these mothers.

Reporting on the Brixton Disorders, Lord Scarman (1981) accepted that there were some police officers who in their dealings on the streets with black people were guilty of immature and racially prejudiced actions. He also pointed out that some of the racism and discrimination against black people was often unconscious, and it remained a major source of social tension and conflict. One of the recommendations in that report was for further training of the police in working with people who were racially and culturally different. Race relations training was given to police, probation and prison services.

The Stephen Lawrence case – a young African Caribbean man, killed by a group of white young men – is an example of this fear, expressed during the early days of the immigration, being realized. The McPherson Report (1999), the result of the inquiry into the case, reported that the issue of racism permeated the inquiry and highlighted the incidence of 'institutional racism' within the police service; in contemporary society there still exists the tension and conflict between police and young black people.

CHILDHOOD EXPERIENCES OF MOTHERS IN THE SAMPLE

In this sample of mothers, 85 per cent were reared by their own mothers. In spite of the 'strictness' about which most of them spoke, and the limited communication between them and their mothers, the childhood of most of the sample, in both groups, was recalled as being happy. In retrospect, those mothers who spoke positively of their childhood experiences felt that their upbringing was 'correct' for them and was a significant factor in the shaping of their characters, and helped them to be the independent and adequate individuals they considered themselves to be. They considered that adherence to certain basic principles such as good manners, respect for older people and obedience to one's parents were necessary in the rearing of children. Some of them recalled their lack of material comforts due to the poverty of their parents, but felt that the poor conditions did not detract from their happiness, because of the close relationships within their families. In other words there was a secure attachment between themselves and their parents.

The mothers who claimed unhappy childhoods described their mothers as not performing their nurturing role, placing the responsibility of caring for their younger siblings on them, and frequently punishing them unfairly. They felt they had been deprived of childhood. They experienced difficulty in the rearing of their children as they were not sure if their ways of doing things were the best for the children.

REARING OF THE CHILDREN

Mrs Layne voiced the opinion of mothers in both groups:

> 'I worry how the children will turn out in this place. I try hard to discipline them but when I see other children doing all sorts of things I feel so scared for mine.'

The mothers in both groups accepted corporal punishment as a way of trying to instil discipline in their children. They wanted them to be seen as having been well reared, and not to exhibit behaviour which would cause parents to feel ashamed in the eyes of an already critical society.

Some mothers spoke of the criticism which was levelled at them by social workers to whom children complained about being 'beaten' (the term used to describe corporal punishment) by their parents.

The impact of social change is always a particularly stressful life event for people of all backgrounds and so it was for the African Caribbean mothers who were trying to cope with adapting to people racially and culturally different from them, different lifestyles and the extreme climatic change. The often hostile and racist reactions to them in all spheres of their lives were hugely unsettling.

Some of the mothers insulated themselves against the strangeness in the society by strict adherence to the old and tried ways of their parents, internalized in their early lives. Some of these, especially in dealing with their adolescent children, did not serve them well and the uncertainty and anxiety of not knowing exactly how to react to various situations became a stressor which in some instances upset their mental health.

PSYCHIATRIC DISORDERS OF MOTHERS

There were two mothers in Group E and one in Group C who had undergone psychiatric treatment. They said that the medicines given were effective in making them feel well again, but feared addiction to the drugs and did not persist in taking them regularly, and expressed the fear of a relapse.

Mrs Skeete had been widowed four years prior to the interview and was finding it difficult to recover from the shock of her husband's sudden death; several factors were contributing to her grief and despair. Her husband had been a caring husband and father. He had purchased a house, seven months before his death, which was in need of repair and because she was now unable to work the repairs could not be done.

Her husband had died the day after they had made the final arrangements for the children left in the Caribbean to join them. In the shock and disorientation caused by the sudden death no thought had been given to requesting the travel arrangements to be advanced in order for the children to arrive before the funeral of their father. This was a source of remorse and guilt.

Mrs Skeete attempted to sew at home but was unable to concentrate as memories of her husband kept crowding in to her thoughts, causing her to collapse in tears. She thought that if she had been able to go out to work, interacting with colleagues might have helped her emotionally. She was further distressed that she was dependent on Social Security benefits and financial help from her two older children and felt that her self esteem was diminished in being dependent on them. Fortunately the relationship with the children was very secure and the children took pride in helping the family to live comfortably together.

Five mothers dwelt upon their lifestyles in their own countries and yearned for the friends and families left behind in the rural areas of their countries, which caused them to feel insecure – in attachment terms they could be considered as disorganized and disorientated. This may have been tinged with some idealization and some spoke of the constant fearful feelings which they experienced as a result of their insecurity.

CONCLUSION

The data collected supported the hypothesis that when mothers and children were separated for long periods it was more difficult for them to relate satisfactorily, especially if the separation occurred during the first three years of the child's life.

The mothers in this study had tried hard to do what they thought was beneficial for their children and some found that too often they were criticized by the indigenous population, lay and professional, for being too restrictive with their children. Some of the children, influenced by their white peer groups who were often allowed a greater measure of freedom, tended to imitate the behaviour of their white peers and rejected the values of their families.

Many of these mothers had felt the need for some supportive service to help them cope with the effects of their loss through the immigration process and that of their children, but lack of knowledge of the systems meant that they did not know to whom they could turn. Often their emotional problems were expressed in physical ailments and they frequented the general practitioners' offices. During the early period of migrants settling in the country, counselling services for the lower socio-economic population was not offered and even if they were it is doubtful whether they would have considered that their needs were being met. Their experience of feeling unwell meant that they expected to be seen by a doctor who would prescribe medicines which were expected to effect a cure.

Some of the mothers were devastated when their reunited children obtained information from their peers about the possibility of being taken into care to live away from their families, and referred themselves to the Social Services. The mothers were even more shocked when some social workers accepted the children as their clients before discussing the situation with them. Feeling humiliated, ashamed and angry, they often withdrew, leaving the care of their children to the government. Thus they and the children grew apart, and the feelings of loss were compounded.

Relationships with social workers and some parents today are often strained and some mothers feel unsupported by social workers whom they see as wielding power which they often use without fully engaging with them to discuss plans for the family. Recently an Appeal Court Judge was reported to have given mothers more time to demonstrate their ability to look after their children. His comments on social workers were: 'They are perceived by many as the arrogant and enthusiastic removers of children from their parents into an unsatisfactory care system and as trampling on the rights of parents and children in the process' (Garner 2010). This emotive generalization, also published in a free paper, *The Metro*, with a wide circulation, serves to foster negative attitudes of the public toward social workers. They find themselves in the situation where they are criticized if they remove children from homes and also if they do not. Nevertheless, there have been instances when some social workers and their supervisors failed to assess the risks of dangers to children and, even when they carried out routine visits to the families, missed important clues that indicated the abuse of children of various ethnic backgrounds, with fatal consequences. For example, clues of prolonged abuse were uncovered following the deaths of two-and-a-half-year-old Jasmine Beckford in 1985 (Blom-Cooper 1985) and eight-year-old Victoria Climbié in 2000 (Laming 2003). Lord Laming's inquiry into Victoria Climbié's death highlighted the fact that several professionals (not only social workers) did not provide the help required to save her from the severe abuse she suffered before her death. In all of the reports of the inquiries into the deaths of the children, several recommendations have been made in the hope that lessons will be learnt and children safeguarded from harm.

The mothers in the sample stressed adherence to the principles which they had internalized during their early childhoods in the Caribbean. These were good manners, obedience to parents, honesty, truthfulness, and respect for older people, a strong work ethic and belief in spirituality. They were critical of some of the practices of the welfare state, which they perceived as encouraging dependency and the feeling that people will be looked after if they do not work. They feared that the boys, especially, would be adversely affected.

The current concern felt by policy makers and by professionals in the field of social care regarding African Caribbean children showing high levels of under-achievement in school, and there being large numbers of African Caribbeans in the social care system and in the criminal justice system as well as many in psychiatric hospitals, seems to confirm the concern of those mothers.

The mothers in the study, like many of the immigrants, did not foresee themselves growing old in Britain. Some prepared for retirement back in the Caribbean by building homes and planned to return after their children had completed their education, whilst others decided to remain and be near to their children and grandchildren and so provide the extended family which they had so greatly missed on coming to Britain. The realization of this will be influenced by the nature of the relationships which they had with their children in their early years.

Although the study concentrated on mothers and the reunions of children who had been left behind, the reactions of fathers are described in the next chapter.

Chapter 5

Fathers in the Reconstituted Families

> Immigration is only one of the issues that will contribute to separation of parent, particularly mother, from child. The socio-cultural context of many Caribbean families suggests that separation of father from child is also a significant issue for many of our children. (Jones, Sharpe and Sogren 2004, p.6)

Many African Caribbean men face issues, for example unemployment, that contribute to their inability to accept the responsibilities of fatherhood and live within a family (Jones, Sharpe and Sogren 2004). There are also some who father several children and are consequently unable to be present in a family. The writings of anthropologists, sociologists and economists about Caribbean families through the decades have highlighted the prevalence of female-headed households in the various countries within the Caribbean region, particularly in families of the lower socio-economic level of society (Clarke 1966; Massiah 1982). It was noted that even when some men were married or co-habiting with the mothers of their children they interacted so little with the family that they still remained marginal to the family (Shorey-Bryan 1986).

One factor which was usually thought to have influenced the pattern of family life was the lasting inheritance of the historical past of slavery. Then, the slave masters assumed responsibility for children born on their plantations and fathers had no influence in the lives of the children (see Chapter 1).

Another reason cited for the absence of men in the family in the post-slavery era was the independence of women who maintained relationships with the fathers of their children but were not in residence with them (Russell-Brown, Norville and Griffiths 1997). This did not mean that the children were deprived of the influence of the father who may very well have interacted with them as much or more than a father in residence.

In the early days of the mass immigration from the Caribbean to Britain, the majority of migrants were men, many of whom were not accompanied by wives or partners. Some of them formed relationships with white women and if they married them the children were included in the migrant group; little information has been found about these families. Nevertheless, there was an unknown number of mixed heritage children who were deserted by the parents and were placed in children's homes (Patterson 1965).

As the immigration progressed and wives and partners joined the men, the nuclear unit was the most common pattern, as members of the extended families had not come in any large numbers. In the 66 families researched (see Chapter 4) 57 were legally married, six families had been broken up through divorce, and one through the death of the husband, and two were single mothers who were not in relationships and had had no contact with the fathers of the children since their pregnancies were discovered. These two mothers were ardent church goers and found social support among the members of the congregation.

Those who had divorced their husbands recalled that the main reason was domestic violence and that even if the violence was not directed against the children, they were adversely affected by the tension in the home. Mothers therefore thought it to be in the children's interest to keep the fathers out of the home.

All of the women considered themselves to be independent as they were in full-time employment; some had furthered their education and often they earned more than their husbands; others did two jobs in order to earn more money to raise their standard of living. They disliked having to leave their children in the care of strangers, that is, child-minders and nursery workers, and where fathers worked on evening shifts, they cared for the children together. This was a change from the pattern among most African Caribbean families who accepted that caring for children was a task which was only performed by women. This active engagement with fathers during the early life of the children provided the opportunity for the development of attachment between them as the following comment from Mrs J indicates:

'My daughter was very close to her father, he looked after her during the day more than I did, as I had to go to work. Sometimes I was upset when she preferred her father to do things for her but she was used to him caring for her.'

APPRECIATION OF FATHERS BY MOTHERS

The support which their husbands gave to mothers in the 'backing up' of the discipline and the sanctions which were imposed on the children, when necessary, was appreciated by the mother, and contributed towards the building of satisfactory relationships within the home.

The following statements were contrary to the stereotype of African Caribbean women who were supposed to be dominant in their households, raising their children with little regard for whether the father was absent or had supported them financially or emotionally.

Mrs G commented that:

'Mothers cannot bring up children alone, much depends on the men to help them.'

Mrs S said:

'The children look up to their dad, and he never lets them down. He takes an interest in everything that they do at school and takes them out to football. That way I do not feel so anxious about them.'

This mother did not use the term 'role model', but the concept was implied and gave a positive image of a father interacting with and taking an interest in his children.

Only three of the mothers with satisfactory relationships with their reunited children were critical of their husbands about economic concerns, but they were not critical of them in the performance of their fathering role. Their criticisms were, for example, the husbands' reluctance to seek more lucrative jobs, or to find better housing, or to share the mothers' desire to move to the USA, where they had heard there were better employment prospects and higher salaries.

It was significant that among those mothers who had unsatisfactory relationships with the children, some were angry with the fathers for being too lenient and for not accepting any responsibility for instilling discipline in the children, especially the boys.

Some of the fathers in the families were uncommunicative and never showed any interest in what other members of the family did, nor in the school activities of the children. These fathers never included the family in any of their leisure activities and mothers did not know what they did nor where they went outside of the home.

The single mothers were unanimous in saying that although they missed the emotional and financial support of the fathers of their children, they considered it better to be alone with the children instead of living with partners with whom they were unable to relate. This they thought would cause tension and conflict in the home and make the children unhappy, and might make them feel obliged to take sides. Some of the mothers who had grown up with fathers in their families, with whom they had related well, expressed the wish that their children could have had similar experiences. This resonates with the findings of a more recent study of mothers' perception of Caribbean men in their families, in which single mothers question their lone mother position, and the well-being of their children in relation to benefits they perceive from a father's 'normative' presence (Reynolds 2005).

Stepfathers

Where there were stepfathers to the reunited children and there were satisfactory relationships among them, mothers were pleased that the children had been accepted by the stepfathers whom they described as 'good fathers'.

Mrs G recalled the plans she made for the reunion for her son:

'I wanted to bring him to further his education, and my mother who was getting old wrote saying that the best place for him was with me. My husband, who is not his father, urged me to send for him. He talks more to his stepfather than to me. I am glad they get on well together.'

Mrs S said:

'Her stepfather treated her as if she was his own child, made no difference at all. Even now she prefers going to him to ask if she wants anything.'

Taking the concept of Internal Working Models into account, it may be that these men, who were able to react so positively towards the children, had satisfactory early experiences with their primary carers and that these influenced their personalities and contributed to their ability to be caring individuals and good fathers.

When stepfathers ignored the children in the family, including those who were reunited, mothers were very perturbed by their lack of communication and by their leaving all the responsibility of caring for the children on them. In trying to preserve their marriages they tolerated the husbands' behaviour.

VIEWS OF CHILDREN REUNITED WITH FAMILIES

The views of children separated from and then reunited with their parents in Britain will be explored in Chapter 6, but their comments on fathers are considered here. When they arrived in Britain, 85 per cent lived in nuclear families and 10 per cent of these had stepfathers; 15 per cent lived with single mothers.

The recollections of the early relationships with their fathers were a mix of positive and negative ones.

Brenda recalled:

> 'My father had a soft spot for me. I did not like pears hard or soft, and he would drive around to find pears that could only be "in between" for my lunch, otherwise I would not eat.'

Ena commented:

> 'My father and I had a close relationship. He was very kind and when I left home for my own place he would be around to do the odd jobs and see to the maintenance.'

Lilian said:

> 'My stepfather was a very quiet person, a kind man. I would go to him for school things rather than ask my mother.'

These women commented that their lasting memories of their fathers/ stepfathers were their kindness and the practical acts done for them, but none spoke of having conversations with them or discussing any matters of any concern to them.

Some recalled that often their fathers and stepfathers mediated between themselves and their mothers, but in other instances, poor relationships between their parents resulted in domestic violence and some of the violence from the father spilled over onto them. They claimed that the latter experiences in their early lives contributed to their reluctance to trust men, and prevented them from entering into any long-term relationships.

Some of the reunited children who joined single mothers regretted that they never met their fathers, or that their mothers never told them anything about them. Others met their fathers when they were adults, but the meetings were casual and no attempt was made to try to relate to each other. Unfortunately, there were instances where some children were the victims of abuse, physical and sexual, by fathers or stepfathers who, not having known them as children in their early years, related to them as sexual partners now they were adolescents. These were traumatic experiences, the memories of which were painful and influenced their decision to remain single.

THE IMAGE OF FATHERS

In recent times some young African Caribbean fathers are speaking out about the persistent stereotypical descriptions of them and are trying to eradicate the image of black fathers as being unreliable, immature, irresponsible and absent from the families. Some of those who do not live with the mother of their children have been able to form satisfactory relationships with them and take care of the children for arranged periods of time, but there are numbers of them who behave irresponsibly and do not support them, or have any relationships with their children.

Several organizations offer programmes for African Caribbean fathers to acquire parenting skills. These are to be welcomed, especially for young men who were alienated from their families and spent most of their childhood in the care system and so missed out on family life in which they might have acquired some child care skills. Unfortunately some of those who would benefit most are reluctant to attend and this may be due to their feelings of inadequacy and low self esteem.

Currently, as a follow-up to care for looked-after children, some adolescents are accommodated for a period of time in units for independent living where their physical needs are met. This is usually provided for adolescents whose relationships with families were unsatisfactory. Some may continue their education, and others may find temporary unskilled jobs, but there is little done to help further their emotional development or preparation for fatherhood and family life.

Most of the debate about fathers in African Caribbean families is about their absence. There are a number of reasons why this may be so, such as being away for employment, serving in the armed forces or being stationed abroad (as was the father of Bowlby). These reasons, whilst causing a measure of family stress, may be better tolerated if the father communicates with the children and if the mother's psychological adjustment helps her to deal with the absence, and permits her to help the children to keep the father in mind. The support of others such as extended family members, friends and appropriate professionals is crucial in helping children to cope when they do not know, and wish to know their fathers, or when fathers are in prison, or in a psychiatric hospital, or when their whereabouts are unknown.

Some children reared by mothers alone, who are themselves secure and stable, have been able to help their own children develop into well-rounded people who appear to be secure and happy in themselves, able to relate to others and who make a worthwhile contribution in society; but when they recall their childhoods many of them express their feelings about the absence of their fathers. Some are dismissive, especially if the father was violent towards their mother and themselves. Others are angry while others are bewildered at the seeming indifference and lack of responsibility exhibited by their fathers.

Many African Caribbean fathers, especially those who hold strong religious beliefs, have contributed positively in their fathering role, and this is seldom acknowledged. There is a need to look beyond the stereotypical images of fathers as portrayed in most of the literature and in the media, and to recognize the variety of fathers that exists, and the extent to which they are committed to their families.

There are some young men who because of unemployment are unable to play their full role as fathers, and in this respect it is as if history is repeating itself, when men in the Caribbean were unable to establish families because of their poor economic status and left the responsibility to the mothers and the maternal extended family.

In contemporary society, many of the British-born young women of African Caribbean origin choose to live independently of the fathers of their children. This seems as if they are carrying on the tradition of female-headed households. In a survey carried out in 2000, it was found that 39 per cent of Caribbean adults under the age of 60 were in formal marriages; among younger people marriage rates were low. Some couples were in 'visiting' partner relationships in which the men accepted paternal responsibilities, but there was a high proportion of young black men who were unemployed and lived alone. In this respect the young men of African Caribbean origin seem to break from the tradition of young men in the Caribbean living in the homes of their parents/mothers until they were financially able to provide a home for themselves and a partner (Berthoud 2000).

Within the last decade, there has been a growing interest in researching Caribbean fatherhood in the Caribbean. The attention given to fatherhood has been described by a group of researchers from the University of the West Indies Jamaica as being 'under researched, and misunderstood', and they refer to some of the literature which 'indicates that many men are participating more fully in the care and nurturing of children and sharing domestic duties with their female partners' (Brown *et al.* 1997, pp.85–6). This was a decided change from earlier times when men did not participate in household chores or help to care for babies and small children.

The practice of mothers having to take responsibility for caring for the children was even extolled in a well-known calypso (a song which made comment on issues of the day), which said that father was going away and if he did not return mother would stay at home and 'mind' (that is, take care of) the baby.

In order to discover male attitudes and behaviours with regard to their families, a survey was undertaken of 700 low-income and working-class men from two urban and two rural communities in Jamaica, and discussions explored the same issues with men and women from similar backgrounds. The results confirmed the well-recorded evidence that many women carried the responsibility of caring for the children without the fathers living in the home. However, there was evidence that men contributed more to family life than that for which they were credited, and that most of them aspired to be good fathers even if they were not always able to carry out their responsibilities as they felt they should. Most of the men saw themselves as not only providing financially for their children, but also generally being good role models for them, interacting with them through play, talking and reasoning with them and helping with their school homework. Approximately half of the sample who lived in the urban areas performed the household tasks of tidying, cooking and shopping at least twice a week, when visiting the household, with more involvement from those living separately from their partners. The researchers found the active parenting other than providing financial support to be a new phenomenon.

Similar positive attitudes and behaviour of African Caribbean men in Britain who are bearing the responsibilities of being fathers are being experienced and these need to be more widely known in order to help to erase the negative stereotypes that are constantly repeated in the media, the literature and in conversations. The men saw being a father as having strong personal meanings for them as it determined how they defined themselves and set them on the path of maturity. They realized that sharing a home with the family was an ideal situation for allowing fathers to influence the children's development, but their understanding of the social and psychological elements considered vital in their development varied widely. The children's relationship with fathers was linked with the relationship between the fathers and the mothers; one third of the sample were dissatisfied with their roles because of mothers refusing to allow them to visit (Brown *et al.* 1997).

Hawkes (2008), writing on the importance of fathers in African Caribbean families in England today, describes her disappointment and frustration when mothers are heard to say 'the children do not need their fathers'. She points out that unless a father is found to be physically abusing in a way that is threatening to life, or seriously abusive psychologically, children have a right to be allowed to have a relationship with their fathers. Some fathers who have abused their children can be helped therapeutically and allowed supervised contact in a safe place where child protection is assured. Hawkes warned young African Caribbean women against accepting the label of 'the strong black woman' which often influenced their attitudes, leading them to refuse to accept support from fathers and deprive their children of contact with them.

Recently men are voicing their feelings of being discriminated against and are prepared to challenge decisions made against them regarding losing or having custody of their children if they and the mothers are no longer in a relationship.

It is frequently lamented that there are few role models for young men of African Caribbean origins in Britain but parents are the first role models and their sensitive caregiving is crucial according to the view proposed by Bowlby (1982a), who stated the importance of relating to the child sensitively so that positive Internal Working Models will develop in the early years of the child and will serve to prepare him or her for future interpersonal experiences.

Chapter 6

African Caribbean Women Reflecting on Separation in their Early Years and Reunion with their Mothers

Children are not slates from which the past can be rubbed by a duster or sponge, but human beings who carry their experiences with them, and whose behaviour in the present is profoundly affected by what has gone before. (Bowlby 1952, p.113)

The emotional wounds caused by the separation and loss of mothers and surrogate mothers in early childhood cannot easily be erased, as Bowlby's (1952) statement suggests.

In this chapter, I present material from interviews with 20 African Caribbean women who were separated from their mothers when they were children. The interviews were carried out using a semi-structured interview schedule (the Separation Reunion Interview Schedule (SRIS)) devised for the study (see Appendix 2). The Interview Schedule was piloted with 11 women before being used in the main study. The aims were to elicit information about how people deal with experiences of separation and loss: whether they cope by acknowledging and confronting difficult emotions or by minimizing and dismissing negative feelings. Using the in-depth interview, it was possible to explore women's internal representations of their mothers and carers, and to find out what meanings they attributed to their early experiences. The women were placed in two groups. Group A, the experimental group, consisted of those who had received or were receiving therapy, and Group B, the control group, had not received therapy. There were ten women in each group.

The 20 interviewees were experiencing difficulty in sustaining relationships in their families of origin. Some were also having similar difficulties in relation to their own families and they all said that they felt low and depressed most of the time. At the time of being interviewed, ten of the women had received psychotherapy or counselling. None of them was familiar either with the psychological findings of psychoanalysts or with the writings of John Bowlby; ten had no experience of therapeutic help. There was little difference in the reactions to the separation-reunion experiences and the importance placed on the effects of these on their present lives. The 20 interview transcripts were remarkably similar, especially with regard to the accounts given of childhood experiences of separation and the importance placed on the effects of this on their current well-being. One opinion which stood out above the rest was that children need to experience a close mother–child relationship in their early lives in order to feel a true sense of self in later life and to prevent 'feeling that something is missing inside'.

Separated when they were infants or toddlers from their mothers who had emigrated to England, the women had been reared mainly by grandmothers; sometimes grandfathers were present, and/or other members of the extended families. After varying periods of time (average 7–8 years) they were subsequently uprooted from their mainly rural homes and brought to Britain to be reunited with mothers who, by then, were strangers. Three quarters of the women were born to young single mothers who lived within extended families in households headed by women. Just under half (45%) were left by their mothers between the ages of one week and three years, a sensitive period in the life of a young child when attachment to the primary carer usually occurs. Over half (55%) were left between the ages of four and six years.

In Britain they lived in isolated nuclear or single parent families in urban towns and cities, in markedly lower-standard living conditions than those they had been accustomed to in their countries in the Caribbean.

The profiles that emerged from the use of the Separation Reunion Interview Schedule were very similar regardless of whether women had been in therapy or not. This was perhaps inevitable, as they had all experienced the losses and the disappointments caused during the migration process. Furthermore their socialization was, in the main, similar within the cultural background of the Caribbean, especially with regard to child shifting and extended family care-giving.

In the sections that follow, women's own words are used to convey the range of feelings about different aspects of separation and reunion, including understanding of why their mother was absent; the difficulty of keeping a memory of mother alive; relationships with the carers with whom they were left; being parted from their carers; being reunited with their mother; relating to other family members; and growing up and living in Britain (school, work, social and adult relationships).

FEELINGS ABOUT WHY THEIR MOTHER WAS NOT THERE

The women who described feeling the most 'confused', as they were growing up, about their mothers' absence tended to be those who had been left at the youngest ages (one week to three years). Some said that their grandmothers had explained that their mothers were away working and that 'it was for the best'. Others, however, commented that such intellectual explanations for mothers' absence did not prevent them from feeling abandoned, nor did intellectual understanding help them to cope with the feelings of abandonment. The following quotes all point to a painful inability to understand why mothers were not there. While some of the women were able to acknowledge how difficult they had found it to cope with their feelings, others denied any sense of hurt or anger.

'I had a different understanding, an unconscious other feeling about it; maybe it was anger, reflection, ideas about love all tied up in it.' (Dora)

'I did not have an understanding of it all; it just made no sense to me. No one questioned: did you feel rejected? Did you want your mum? But they reminded you that you should not be an ungrateful child, your Mum was doing the best, and you should accept. They did not know better, I suppose, it wasn't made much of, so I suppose I did not give feelings much thought.' (Sylvia)

'I never missed her, I never thought about her or in my mind wondered what Mum is doing or when I am going to see my mum. You know they say: what you never had you don't miss. My mother just dumped me and probably did not think about me until she wanted me to come here.' (Lilian)

Esther reflected on having to suppress feelings maybe linked to a cultural history of slavery and oppression:

> 'The emotional side was kind of historical [i.e. emotions being felt now stem from the memory of the slave experience of black people]; it was not something that aided survival in our case. It was about survival. You could not start lying down and saying, "I am not loved," there was no time for that. Maybe that is just passed on [i.e. repression of emotions]. I think the emotional side gets ignored.'

THE LACK OF AN IMAGE OF MOTHERS

A small number of the women said that they were aware that their grandmothers were not their mothers as they told them their mothers were abroad, but others believed that their grandmothers were their mothers. Some of the women had been shown photographs of their mothers, but those who hadn't were unable to form an image of them. For some it was as if a mother had never existed.

> 'I have no image of my mother. None at all.' (Eva)

> 'I do not know at what age I was left, I have no memory of ever calling anyone mother.' (Shirley)

> 'I met my mother when I was nearly ten years old and as far as I can remember I had never seen this woman before in my life.' (Lana)

> 'I was about two years old when my mother left. There were photographs of her but I did not ask any questions about her. The only thing my thoughts of her were related to was receiving presents.' (Ruby)

When the women tried to recall whether they had an image of their mothers during their childhood, they found it impossible to do so. They attributed this to being engrossed in their lives with their carers and peers. Most recalled that when they arrived in England, their mothers were complete strangers to them. Their mothers did not know them as they had missed out on their growing years.

'Even as much as mothers here want it, the connection isn't there. There is no bonding; there is no relationship, nothing at all. For all that the child knows, the only mother or father is either grandmother or grandfather or aunt.' (Anna)

Sylvia, who was dismissive about not thinking about feelings, expressed the view:

'Because so many of my friends at school had their mothers in England, it was like nothing out of the ordinary.'

This dismissive attitude may have served to help her to cope with knowing that her grandmother was not her mother for whom she must have been grieving, and she may have cultivated this attitude as a defence mechanism against the pain she felt. It was no surprise that the pattern of attachment developed into one of insecure and avoidant.

WITH WHOM THEY WERE LEFT

Seventy-five per cent of the women were left with maternal grandmothers, 15 per cent with paternal grandmothers, 5 per cent with a maternal aunt and 5 per cent with a godmother. The majority spoke of happy childhood years with carers in the extended family.

'My sister and I were treated much better than the other children in the family because our parents were sending money for us.' (Ellen)

'I was the only young little girl; there were other bigger ones so I didn't do very much, just played.' (Florence)

'My grandmother taught me respect for people in the family and how to perform household chores. I think I see her as my mentor really, she is the one I remember as the person who instilled all the values I hold in me.' (Edith)

Not all were so happy and comfortable. Dora was left with a grandfather and an aunt. She was still very sad when she recalled her early childhood:

'If I am honest with you, I have to say those years were hard.'

She was unable to describe the hardships.

Ruby described her grandmother's house as being like an orphanage. All of her aunts who had migrated had left their children to be cared for in that household:

> 'My grandmother had too many children to look after; there was not enough love to go around, and I felt left out.'

PREPARATION FOR LEAVING CARERS

Some of them were prepared for leaving:

> 'My great aunt sat me down and told me I was going to meet my mother and I should call her "Mum" and call my stepfather "Dad". I should be a good girl and I shouldn't mix with people who were bad, for people judge you by the people that you mix with. I knew that it was going to be cold, and that it was going to be different, and there were a sister and a brother.' (Dora)

Fifteen of the women recalled that they were unprepared for leaving their carers:

> 'They did not ask if I wanted to go to England. There was no explanation really, just that I was going up to meet my mum.'

> 'In those days, nobody cared about a child's feelings or what you were going to go through; your parents need you and you have to go.'

> 'It was not dealt with properly. My sister and I didn't know what was happening. I felt like we were going to town and we were going to see our grandmother again. I can never understand why we never saw her again. It has taken me years to realize we never saw her again, how horrible that was. I used to dream about her for years and years.'

Reflecting on this lack of preparation, most of the women accepted that it was the cultural norm that children were not consulted on matters which were considered the responsibilities of adults. Since they trusted their grandmothers they accepted what was said to them. The feelings of children were not considered and the need to say goodbye and mourn the loss of a loved one was not recognized. It was noticeable that what was thought necessary in the preparation was to remind them of moral values, and to teach them practical skills.

In some instances, a grandmother or an aunt accompanied them, or mothers returned home to bring them back to England, but there was no preparation for the change in the physical appearance of the country and the change of climate. Those whose mothers had not sent suitable clothing for the cold weather arrived in England inadequately dressed in flimsy summer clothes and sandals, but some were given a warm coat on arrival.

MEETINGS WITH MOTHERS

Seventy-five per cent of children did not recognize their mothers, and mothers seemed unable to greet the children. Of the 25 per cent who recognized them, one woman remembered that she went straight up to her mother and hugged and kissed her as she had recognized her from photographs, but the majority related a tense meeting which lacked any emotion.

> 'I had no recollection of who she was, and I had a confusion because I had sisters who were big people and when I arrived a sister seemed interested in me. My mother never made a fuss of me.' (Cynthia)

> 'I saw pictures of her so I knew her physical appearance but I didn't know her. I was ambivalent; I felt this, you know, want to hug and not want to hug, but my mother was very warm and wanted to hug. I could not understand why my body fell towards her and back from her.' (Dora)

> 'I cannot remember my mother holding me, and there was silence all the way from the airport; I cried all the way and nobody said anything.' (Anna)

The lack of holding when they arrived was mentioned by 17 (85%) of the women. The reunited children were afraid of the new situation and their anxiety was not recognized.

The comments indicated that there was disappointment with the initial contact with mothers who showed no emotion and no ability to comfort them. Some of the children had fantasized that the person who sent money and parcels of clothes must be rich. They found that in some instances mothers were not well dressed and they were disappointed and disillusioned. As noted in Chapter 4, they were reluctant to address their mothers as 'Mum' as they had been used to using that name for their grandmothers.

Ninety-five per cent of the women were disappointed with the reception they received from mothers, and even when some mothers tried hard to greet them with love and affection, the children seemed impervious to demonstrations of love and affection. As one recalled:

> 'I remember she was hugging us and saying, "They are over here at last, I have my children." I just put up with it really; it was really nice but I was more impressed with all the sweets she had packed up for us. I remember her crying and hugging us but I cannot remember thinking "Oh, this is my mum," I just thought she was a strange woman.'

RELATIONSHIPS WITH MEMBERS OF THE NEW FAMILY

Eighty-five per cent of the women lived in nuclear families and in 10 per cent of these there were stepfathers. Fifteen per cent lived with single mothers. In both groups, life with their mothers was problematic. They were in the main disappointed that there was no caring and nurturing. Communication by the mother was usually in the form of 'do this, do that'; there was never 'thank you' or 'well done'.

Ninety-five per cent of the women reported physical punishment. They knew that it was the norm among Caribbean families but they felt that in most cases the punishment was unjustified.

> 'I had this idealized mother; this mother who would never smack me, everything my grandmother did of course, this mother would never do. You must realize she was totally perfect in my mind. She would not tell me off or anything like that. It was totally unrealistic, and a big job she had to live up to in my mind. Then one day she hit me. That just about blew this concept and I felt totally rejected because she did not fit into the image I had of "mother". She would never hit me, this mother, and she hit me harder than my grandmother who very rarely hit me and she hit me harder. So I loved her and hated her all at one time, ambivalent, really ambivalent.' (Florence)

'With my mother it was like head-on war with me; it was like I was her in some ways. It was like she looked at me and she looked at herself so she would always hit me and she never hit my sister. I would just antagonize my mother because she just shattered the concept of the mother I had in my head, I would never cry. With those people you must cry. If you want the beating to stop you must cry. With me I was stubborn as a mule, I would not cry, didn't matter how much she hit me I would not cry, which made her beat me more.' (Becky)

Some recalled how unjustifiable the punishments were:

'My mother never found out why I was in a fight at school. She used to say "I didn't send you to school to fight" and I would say that it was not my fault. My mother did not want to know, and would say "You have to rise above it, you know that will happen in life, just get on with it." She just wanted me to take it and I just couldn't do that.' (Lilian)

'I wasn't bad or naughty, but if I did not do things on time I was beaten. It was bad and she beat me with anything she found. I suppose in today's terms I was physically abused, it was too bad.' (Ada)

In spite of the hurt and humiliation she felt when punished, Vera was forgiving of her mother and excused her in the following words:

'It was because of my mum's stress and I think impatience and lack of sleep. She didn't do it knowingly, just felt that she was keeping discipline or I would go haywire like all those other girls.'

Some accepted the punishment during the early years but some eventually stood up to their mothers. More often, they decided to leave home and found work and furthered their education. Some selected nursing where student hostels provided secure accommodation. Others stayed with friends whose families were sympathetic to them.

In spite of knowing that it was the cultural norm in the West Indies that children were physically punished, the women regarded their punishment as excessive and unfair since in most instances the younger siblings were not physically punished. The women recalled their anger and resentment at this treatment, which they thought served to erode their self esteem.

Communication between most of the mothers and reunited children was minimal, and where this was so, there was an uncomfortable environment, which did not facilitate the establishing of relationships.

RELATIONSHIPS WITH FATHERS AND STEPFATHERS

The fathers were also strangers to the children when they arrived. The majority had been cared for in households headed by women and in some instances the fathers had left when they were young children and so they had no memories of them. Some of the women commented on the kindness of their fathers and stepfathers, while others had difficult relationships.

> 'Very often it was my father who would stop my mother from going on at me. He was quiet.' (Delia)

> 'He was autocratic and always looked for a reason to beat you, what you did or what you didn't do.' (Esther)

Fathers did not communicate very much, but they met the children's material needs. Some fathers also physically punished them and in two instances one father and one stepfather sexually abused them. Because of poor relationships with their mothers they were unable to speak about the abuse and as soon as they left school they left home.

RELATIONSHIPS WITH SIBLINGS

It was difficult for those reunited children who had been the youngest ones in the centre of the extended family, when in the Caribbean, to find themselves marginal to the new household and yet playing a responsible role of looking after their young siblings and performing most of the household tasks. From experiences in the Caribbean, they expected respect from the younger children. When they reprimanded them, mothers objected with harsh words such as 'They are better than you.'

This comment may have arisen out of an internalization of the belief in the superiority of the English and appears to be illogical, since they were the same parents, but they regarded the children born in England as superior to the children born and reared in the Caribbean. For many of the women their perceptions were that their mothers showed preference for and loved the younger children more than them. This was inevitable since mothers and the younger children had become attached to each other. When the young siblings became offensive and asked them why they did not go back to where they had come from or why they had come to live in their house, mothers never reprimanded them. This was extremely painful and confusing as it was deviating from the cultural norm of younger children showing respect to their older siblings who were often their surrogate mothers.

If the younger children were told about the reunited child and were prepared for them joining the family the problems of disrespect did not occur. When the younger children were born after the reunited child arrived it was much easier for the children, as Florence said:

> 'I was very pleased to have younger siblings and enjoyed caring for them. By the time they were born I had adjusted to my new surroundings, had made friends at school and even though I missed my grandmother, I had come to the realization that there was no going back. I felt that I could channel the love I received from my grandmother into caring for them.'

It was as though this was an attempt to demonstrate good child care to her mother.

RELATIONSHIP WITH SCHOOL

Seventy-five per cent of the women recalled their unhappiness at school where very often they were ridiculed for their accents and discriminated against on the basis of being black. Some retaliated and dealt with their tormentors by fighting. Some recalled that they finally left school with CSEs (Certificates of Secondary Education – school leaving qualifications, which were recognized as being less academic than O Levels) because all the black girls were put in CSE classes, and there was the tendency for teachers to steer black children into sport.

> 'I can remember fighting a lot. At school, I would be teased and called names so I hit them and they would hit me back. Therefore, I would fight with them. I was good at fighting and I was the biggest girl in my primary school so I could easily win.' (Florence)

'School was very uncomfortable and I was not happy there. The teachers refused to accept that I knew enough to be placed in the class that was appropriate for me. I played tennis very well but the sports teacher refused to put me on the team and tried to channel me into athletics. I refused to run. I finally left the school and was admitted to a college of further education where I sat and passed O levels.' (Lana)

The negative attitudes of the teachers were recalled by most of the women. These attitudes were not surprising when placed in the political context of the time. Restrictions on entry to Britain were being placed on black immigrants who had previously had the right to enter the country, having been British subjects during the colonial period. And some parents were experiencing difficulty in bringing their children to join them. Racism was more openly displayed than it is now, not only by individuals but also within the institutions. (Things were similar to the circumstances described in Chapter 3; though some time had elapsed, there was little change in attitudes towards black migrants.) However, some of the women recalled positive experiences at school.

'I loved school, it was an escape. It was so much more relaxed over here. Nobody sat down in rows and recited the tables; they just left it and I didn't learn anything in junior school. I didn't learn anything new. It was only when I went to the comprehensive school that I think I actually learnt because I had adjusted to being over here by then. My qualifications when I left, I got four CSEs.' (Lilian)

'I enjoyed school. It was a place where I felt good. I had many friends among my peers and most of the teachers were good to me. I had good grades in CSEs, but was not encouraged by my parents to continue studying.' (Ena)

Nevertheless, Ena was determined to become a nurse, and attended evening classes and obtained the required number of O levels in order to apply to a hospital for training.

'I enjoyed school but was not as inspired as at school back in the Caribbean. I found all I had to do was sit down and smile and talk. I went into regression, didn't do anything, then one day I just woke up and I thought again; I was responsible for myself.' (Greta)

Greta was fortunate that the headmistress of that school had a positive attitude towards the immigrant children. When the subject teachers wanted to advise her against taking the courses she wanted, she appealed to the headmistress who told her that if she wanted to do something, she could do it and she was registered for the courses she wanted. This was not the experience of many.

Most of the women who succeeded at school were those who had joined their parents when they were older and had a grounding in schools in the Caribbean which at the time followed the curriculum of schools in England. For those who were not encouraged by mothers to stay on at school this was confusing as they had been led to believe that to provide education for them was one of the reasons parents had migrated, and it was considered to be the route to their social and economic advancement.

This lack of encouragement by mothers mainly occurred with those with unsatisfactory relationships; the reasons why they did not encourage the children to continue studying are open to conjecture. In some instances the family was disadvantaged by poverty even though parents were employed, and progress out of the poverty trap was slow. With little in the way of social life they relied on relationships at work to avoid isolation, and may have thought this was a way for their children to go. There may have been some who thought they had sacrificed enough through all the early years of the children's lives in the Caribbean by sending remittances and it was time for them to be assisted by the grown children; besides, they were still sending money for the support of their extended families back home and were finding difficulty in maintaining two families. Whatever the reasons, this only served to widen the gap between themselves and their children.

Twelve of the women continued their education and became graduates, three in Group A and nine in Group B. They attributed their determination to succeed to having modelled their behaviour on that of their primary carers, mainly their grandmothers. Their interactions with positive primary carers in the extended family in the Caribbean contributed to their ambitious feelings and desire to achieve. For some, it seemed that to achieve academically was to demonstrate to mothers that in spite of being rejected in favour of their younger siblings born in England, and being hampered with all of the domestic chores and little time to study during their early years, they had succeeded.

Relationships with peers in college were satisfactory but some of the women remarked that they always felt they were not 'as good' as the other students, especially in communication. This low self esteem could have sprung from the poor relationships with their mothers and the frequent derisory remarks made to them about their accents and their Caribbean identification. There was no 'secure base' to which they were able to return and discuss their concerns and be encouraged and praised.

On my remarking to one of the women that in spite of the difficulty in relating to her mother, one of the aims of mothers migrating to England was to help their children to receive a high standard of education to enable them to enter one or other of the professions, and that she had achieved this, she replied:

> 'I have achieved educationally but at what emotional cost? I am not wholly right inside.'

She said this placing her hand on her heart. This may be interpreted as feeling disconnected and not experiencing an attachment with her mother. This she had experienced with her grandmother and there was grief, which she had not been helped to mourn after leaving her.

WORK RELATIONSHIPS

Work was important and liberating for the women in both groups and all were employed. Seventy-five per cent had left home, found accommodation with friends and started to work in a variety of jobs immediately after leaving school. Some worked in shops, some did clerical work, some worked in care homes, and one joined the army. Their main purpose in finding employment was to separate from the family. Some who entered nursing lived in hostels as far away from home as possible.

Their representational models of their mothers were of hard-working women, often working at two jobs in order to maintain what they considered a reasonable standard of living, but the women were determined that they would not adopt the work patterns of their mothers. Ethel claimed that she had no memory of herself as a baby:

> 'I felt there was something inside of me that had to care for babies. I think I was about 21 years old before I stopped feeling that I had to constantly care for this baby inside of me. I knew there was something I was looking for. As I said there was no

knowledge about me, no concept of me as a baby so I was fascinated with babies.'

RELATIONSHIPS WITH PARTNERS

Thirty per cent of the women in the sample had married but 50 per cent of these unions had ended in divorce. Twenty-five per cent of the husbands had had similar experiences of separation from and reunion with their mothers and seemed to have been traumatized as well. One woman remarked that her husband seemed to have suffered more than she did as he had no siblings left with him who could have helped him, when reunited in the new family, with recalling memories of life with the extended family. They all experienced their husbands as very needy, casting their wives in the role of mothers and competing with the children for attention. One of the women, whose husband was ethnically different from her, thought that she was lacking in trust and so did not believe that she was really wanted for herself but only as the mother of their children. When they parted, her husband kept the children. She bore other children from other partners and cared for them but was not able to sustain relationships as she always felt that she was not really wanted by the men in her life. She cared for the children from the unions subsequent to her marriage without help from their fathers.

Some women were reluctant to enter partnerships for a number of reasons. Some observed their mothers in difficult relationships with uncaring partners. Others thought the men they had met were too controlling; some were threatening violence, and others had had similar childhood experiences and were still working through their traumatic loss and reunion issues; others were unable to trust anyone.

> 'I may have had a long-lasting relationship with my kid's dad, but it was from my stepdad that I realised the expectations that men had of women, and that put me off wishing to enter a relationship. I told my partner "If you want to be with me meet me halfway, if you don't, just go."' (Sylvia)

> 'What I have found is that the men with whom I had come in contact seemed to want to take on the role of my mum to manipulate me. There was one with whom I thought I'd have made a relationship but he was threatening and used violent abusive language.' (Dora)

Laura expressed her attitude to relationships as follows:

> 'I don't have that sense of trust, of getting close and trusting, so there is always a part of me that knows that I am staying back and keeping back. I hug, but I am also withdrawing as well at the same time.'

She had had proposals of marriage but considered it impossible to imagine the person around her for any length of time. She described the fear she experienced when she thought of marriage and children and her inability to entertain the concept of being attached to anyone for a length of time. She felt self sufficient and was deeply involved in her work in an office where no close personal relationship was expected.

Two of the women, both in Group B, whose marriages were intact said that their husbands were compatible and understanding. One thought that she had taken her father as a model. The other, whose husband was from the indigenous population, thought that their similar interests had been a cementing factor in their marriage.

Of those who were single, one said that she had never met anyone who lived up to the standards of her father:

> 'He was the model for me, kind and helpful.'

The other two women seemed unsure of their sexuality. They had experienced heterosexual relationships but these were not sustained. Neither was in a same-sex partnership. One of the women, who had finally accepted that she was a lesbian, reflecting on how her mother would react to the knowledge of her sexuality, said:

> 'She would never be able to accept it as she had strong religious beliefs.'

Listening to the narratives of the women in the sample, it seemed that their psychosocial development had been undermined. Their adolescence and early adulthood had been turbulent, traumatic and lonely when the development of identity and intimacy with peer groups would have been developing. They had not been able to share being themselves and were unable to lose and find themselves in others and experience 'a favourable outcome of devotion and fidelity, affiliation and love' (Erikson 1963, p.274).

THE WOMEN'S ENCOUNTERS WITH RACISM

The women who came to Britain as children had lived in the rural areas of their countries in the Caribbean where black people were in the majority. Their teachers in their infant and primary schools were black and black politicians had taken some of the countries from colonial status to independence, so they were aware that black people were capable of wielding power.

Arriving in England, the children realized that their parents were in a minority and being discriminated against, especially in employment and housing. They were very often living in very poor circumstances and working long hours in menial jobs. The children's fantasies of wealthy parents living in big houses and providing material comforts were soon shattered and they found themselves indirectly victims of the racism suffered by their parents.

Direct racism was experienced on the streets where they were subjected to being called racist names, and in schools where their accents were ridiculed, and teachers had low expectations of their abilities which often prevented them from achieving. Some were placed in classes where the standard of work was below that of the school they had left in the Caribbean.

Since some black athletes here in Britain had shown remarkable prowess on the sports field, some of the children found themselves pressed to fit the stereotype of being good at sport to the exclusion of academic studies. The careers officers also treated the black children less well in helping them to make choices; they often refused to discuss their choices with them and gave them information for lower status jobs whilst white girls had 'nice interesting careers'.

One of the women described her refusal of the advice given to her to be a typist rather than a teacher; she used her initiative and gained admission to a college where she was able to achieve her aim. She concluded her reflection by saying:

> 'Black children were not badly behaved at that time in class, but after a time as we got further up the fifth year I think we just got fed up with the way we were treated. One girl taunted the teachers a bit, and most of the black children were expelled the year before we were due to take exams. Fortunately I was not expelled. It was really painful stuff.'

The parents were amazed that it was possible for children to be expelled from school, as they had come from the Caribbean where the English system of education had been made compulsory and so children were kept in school no matter what. They also had a close relationship with teachers especially in the rural areas and were able to discuss their children's progress and behaviour. Parents also felt ashamed that their children's behaviour had been the cause of their exclusion and so had confirmed some of the negative and discriminatory attitudes against black people. Some of the mothers who did not know the systems, or were not sufficiently secure to confront the situation, did not question the teachers' decisions. Some of the girls, depending on their ages, just drifted into casual dead end jobs, whilst others went on to further their studies.

None of the women talked of blatant racism at work but they were aware that racism was endemic in society and were always alert to when it would impact on their lives. This constant watchfulness created stress and further hampered their ability to trust people generally.

STRESS AND ADAPTATION

In Britain over the past decades there has been considerable debate about mental health diagnoses for African Caribbean people. Little or no attention had been paid to the impact of broken attachments and the stresses of reunification of families with children separated for several years. The women of the sample who joined families have employed various strategies to cope with stress in the strange environment.

Some of them, in spite of not having been encouraged by parents to further their education, recalled that their grandmothers always instilled in them the need for education in order to progress in the world. They channelled their energies into educational achievement and excelled in their work which was mainly in the caring professions or teaching.

Most of the children who had been left at an early age in the care of grandmothers and extended families retained strong feelings of identification with their Caribbean origins. The early positive relationships had given them a solid base which assisted them to survive as adults in the face of frustrations and adversity even when they were unable to sustain long-lasting relationships. Conversely, the women whose early relationships with primary carers were negative, and who were unable to relate to mothers when they were reunited, found difficulty in coping with their lives. These were the ones who felt low and depressed most of the time. One woman, who had attempted suicide, expressed the view that there was no point in living if you were rejected by your family.

DISAPPOINTMENT

A theme which reoccurred was the disappointment in every aspect of the reunion experience for most of the women. Their fantasies of their mothers being rich had been encouraged when as children in the Caribbean money and parcels were sent from England to their families. They were particularly disappointed with not being nurtured by their mothers as most of them were by their grandmothers, and those who had been neglected by their surrogate carers had hoped to be shown love and affection from their mothers when they were reunited.

England was a disappointment; it was grey and cold most of the time and the buildings made of stone were associated with factories or prisons in their home countries. Often their homes were very limited and less well appointed than those they had left in the Caribbean.

Schafer (1999, p.1093) claimed that 'disappointment is an inevitable, pervasive, more or less painful, and perhaps traumatic experience in almost every phase of life'. The accumulated disappointments which most of the women experienced in their early years in reconstituted families seem to have developed in them a state of what Schafer named 'disappointedness'.

Most of the women were convinced of the correlation between broken attachments in their early lives and their inability to trust others. They feared that they would be hurt and rejected again and have the pain of their early lives revived. Those whose partners had undergone the separation-reunion experience were doubly disadvantaged. They acknowledged that neither of them had developed trust and that they had similar unmet needs, and therefore the relationship could not be sustained.

RESILIENCE

Some of the women possessed a keen sense of humour, were temperamentally easy-going and had developed strategies for dealing with problems so as to prevent too much frustration and stress in their lives. They seemed to fit the definition of a resilient person as 'one who bounces back having endured adversity or who continues to function reasonably well despite continued exposure to risk' (Gillian 1997).

Gillian (1997), writing in the context of planning for permanence in the arrangements of placing children in adoptive homes, discusses three building blocks of resilience, namely:

• the child's sense of a secure base

• the child's self esteem

• the child's sense of self efficacy.

This framework is relevant in the examination of the resilient behaviour of these women. They had been reunited with their mothers/parents in an attempt to provide permanence within the homes of their biological parents. For those whose reunions had failed, the women had created secure bases for themselves and felt supported by their social networks and some by compatible partners.

The analysis of the interviews with the women identified some issues which shaped their lives after meeting their parents in England and highlighted some of the reasons why reunion was in some instances traumatic:

• The separation, which meant that as children the women had very scant memories of mothers/parents who were for most of them strangers when they met. They had become attached to their primary carers, that is, grandmothers and other members of the extended family, during their early years in the West Indies.

• The expectation by mothers that the reunited children would love them and accept the rules and culture of the household, which included fathers/stepfathers and siblings who were strangers to them.

• Lack of preparation of the children and mothers for the reunion. Preparation could have alerted them to the feelings of being strangers when they met.

• The loss of communication with grandmothers and extended family and the lack of encouragement to relate their memories of early childhood to anyone in their new family.

• The responsibility which was thrust upon the reunited children for looking after younger siblings who very often resented their presence. This was more often than not a new role as back in the West Indies they had been the favoured ones and were looked after by their grandmother and other members of the extended family.

- Schools were the main source of the children's contact with society and for most of them the experiences there were negative. Their speech, which was for the most part in dialect, their accents and their teachers' accents were variables which presented problems of understanding and communication between them.

- Racist words which as they had never heard them before, left them confused and hurt.

- Housing: for some, their homes were uncomfortable. Coming from tropical countries where open windows and doors were the norm, the confined space of a flat or terraced house was constrictive.

- As explained in Chapter 2, black families had been assigned the council's least desirable accommodation and often there was multiple occupancy with the other residents sharing the kitchen and bathroom which were considered private spaces. When families bought houses these were in a state of disrepair, therefore physical comforts were often missing.

- Because of discrimination in the employment of black migrants, mothers worked in poorly paid jobs and often felt it necessary to work in several jobs in order for the family to be financially viable. It was therefore difficult for mothers to spend time with children even to sit and share a meal.

- The churches, which many of the migrants thought would have been welcoming, in most places were not. In the Caribbean, attendance at church was not only regarded as important for spiritual reasons but also served as a meeting point with friends. In Britain, attendance became less frequent as black people experienced hostility or indifference and so they ceased to attend, thus depriving children of another custom which had been part of their lives in their home countries.

When the young women left home and established their own families, some became involved in the non-conformist churches. There, they felt supported and experienced a sense of belonging; those with talents in music and preaching found opportunities to develop these.

Some of the women in Group B (who were not in counselling/therapy) claimed that their strong faith and active worshipping contributed to their ability to cope with the pain of having poor family relationships, and they have progressed into having satisfactory relationships in their own families. Others have not been so fortunate, with some of them again experiencing separation and loss, this time the loss of their children in the care system because of their inability to parent them.

CONCLUSION

The actual experience of separation alone does not determine emotional or psychological outcomes, but the context and quality of the separation and reunion as well as other factors such as ill health, abuse or unequal treatment in the family and in the wider society do contribute to these outcomes (Thomas 2001). Some of these factors were poor housing and poor schools in degenerate areas, racial discrimination which served to determine the employment offered and their promotion within the jobs, over-vigilance by the police service, and victimization on the street. These were traumatizing and seemed to enclose some individuals in a vicious circle from which generations seem unable to escape.

According to Herman (1992), trauma can produce such feelings of helplessness, fear and threat of annihilation that those states of mind are capable of causing the disorganization of mental functioning and prevent the adaptations that ordinarily provide a sense of control and meaning. Some members of African Caribbean families seem to be still suffering from the trauma of fractured lives experienced in early childhood and suffer the long-lasting grief and anger, effects of separation and loss, which have not been processed and resolved.

Some did not seek help from the caring professions voluntarily, either because they were unaware of the existence of therapeutic services, or because they could not afford to pay for the services, and some became so depressed that eventually they were admitted to psychiatric hospitals. In some instances the diagnosis of mental illness, especially schizophrenia, was dubious.

It has been of concern among those working in the field of mental health among black and ethnic minority clients that schizophrenia is over-diagnosed among second generations of African Caribbean men and women born in Britain (Littlewood 2000). Some attribute this to the stresses of the new society, the accumulation of racist incidents, the loss of relationships of extended families and feelings of not belonging, which contribute to mental illness.

Over the years there have been several changes which have been instrumental in making lives less stressful for some families but it is disappointing that some of the issues present at the time of the research continue to be unresolved. These are highlighted in the following chapter.

Chapter 7

Implications for Work with African Caribbean Families

The historical background of this book was considered necessary for working with African Caribbean families who very often are subjected to inadequate services as a result of assessments made and decisions taken based on mythological and stereotypical inaccuracies.

Some of the problems which some families encountered during the early years of immigration when they were strangers to Britain have been stated by first and second generations of African Caribbean people themselves. There are now third and fourth generations of people of African Caribbean origin, some of whom identify themselves as British, seeing no difference between their ideals and those of their white peers, but they are often treated as though they are immigrants. Others describe themselves as feeling they do not belong to Britain but are unable to identify with the birth places in the Caribbean of their parents and therefore feel a sense of detachment. If people are unable to relate to their environment with ease the chances are that this feeling of unease and unbelonging can affect their emotional health. This was a problem in the early days of the immigration and there are certain specific issues which contributed to the feelings.

HOUSING

One of the biggest problems was housing and today, several decades later, a disproportionate number of black families are still living in some of the poorest inner-city areas. People of African Caribbean origins, together with black Africans from other ethnic groups, are least likely to own the property in which they live (Department for Communities and Local Government 2008).

Today some families own their own houses and some rent from Housing Associations. One positive step forward is that black and ethnic minority people have become involved in Housing Association activity and though this is still in a small way it has given minority ethnic people opportunities to participate in the provision of housing.

Coming from mainly rural areas of the Caribbean with close networks of family and friends, many of the immigrants experienced difficulty in adapting to rearing children in England's inner cities where in some areas there are high crime rates and poor schools. Some families who are financially able have left the inner cities to find more domestic space elsewhere, but not all live comfortably in the predominantly white communities where, among white families, they, along with others who move into the area, are seen as not belonging. Friendships are often forged between these groups but seldom with the local people. Very often, racism is blatantly and persistently directed against them and their children; as the incidents mount up over time, this can have long-term negative effects on the individuals' feelings of self esteem and on their mental health.

Some young people in contemporary society, when they do not conform to the standards set by their parents, tend to leave home believing that if they are homeless they will be helped through the social services to obtain housing.

In 2006 the Commission for Racial Equality issued a code of practice on racial equality in housing which replaced codes issued in the early 1990s. It noted that black and minority ethnic communities are up to three times more likely to be represented in statistics on homelessness and, in some areas, racial harassment is seen as four times more likely than in white households (Commission for Racial Equality 2006). In this respect, little has changed.

Home and housing have an important influence on the lives of individuals. Feelings of insecurity and threats to personal safety can contribute to poor mental health in children and adults, preventing them from making healthy relationships and living fulfilled lives.

EDUCATION

When African Caribbean families first came to Britain there were small numbers of children of school age in the families and therefore black children were a minority in schools, but over the decades school populations have changed. There are now schools in a fifth of education authorities in England where black and ethnic minority children outnumber white British children (Paton 2007). Is this due to the flight of white residents when immigrant families moved into the area (as discussed in Chapter 2)? The media reports on failing schools where a large proportion of children are unable to read and write properly at age 14. Recently they are more positive in reporting as some of these schools have been turned around by enthusiastic headteachers, some of whom are of African Caribbean origins.

Some families have sent their children to private schools where they anticipate that the environment of the school will be more conducive to learning and their children will be better taught in smaller classes.

Although there are children who have achieved well in school and have progressed to tertiary education and done well at universities, reports down the years have shown that the educational attainment of African Caribbean boys lags behind that of the girls and that of other ethnic groups. The boys are also found in the groups of children with the highest rate of exclusion from school, along with Gypsy/Roma people and Travellers of Irish Heritage; African Caribbeans are three times more likely to be permanently excluded than the whole school population (DCSF 2009). On the other hand, when non-achieving children are removed to schools with teachers who do not hold stereotypical views of low achievement of black children, and who communicate to children and parents that they have high expectations of them, the outcomes are positive. There are some schools where some black parents are school governors, they participate in parent–teacher meetings which are held at times suitable for working parents, and they are mentors for children who benefit from individual attention to their needs.

Over the decades Saturday Schools have continued to thrive. These were established early in the days when African Caribbean children were not progressing in state schools and numbers of them were being labelled educationally subnormal. When parents realized that their children were not being specially helped but stigmatized and were not likely to return to mainstream schools they and teachers, psychologists and social workers of African origin who had been educated in the Caribbean (and some had taught there) decided to provide tuition to supplement that of the state schools. Saturday Schools have been successful in retaining some of these children who have been excluded and are effective in their teaching methods with them. They are also beneficial to parents who feel supported. Beverley Goring (2004) draws attention to the scarcity of research which gauges the issues around education from 'a more focussed Caribbean parental perspective that analyses the myriad strategies parents employ in relation to their concerns about education' (p.16).

Goring also suggests that research which highlights the experiences and the issues which are now important to contemporary parents and their interaction with the education system in the twenty-first century would add to the debate on education and the African Caribbean child.

It seems that the issues around the ability of African Caribbean children to learn has shifted to issues around behaviour and discipline. Parents feel that they are no longer able to discipline their children who are made aware of their rights, and they also feel that the schools are too lax in setting boundaries for children. They also blame the familiarity which permits children to call teachers by their first names and see this as a lack of respect for people older than themselves and people in authority. When teachers ignore little misdemeanours children will stretch the boundaries and this may lead to exclusion.

Many children of all ethnic groups who experience problems of an emotional nature present with conduct disorders in the classroom and on the playground. Their behaviour can be considered so disruptive and challenging to teachers that they are excluded. Among these there is a disproportionate number who are of African Caribbean origin.

Arnold and Geddes (2004) present a factor which may have affected many African Caribbean families who have experienced separation and loss as described in this book. It is proposed that the impact of separation and losses associated with migration and reunion involving insecure attachments has resulted in an intergenerational influence which affects children of current generations. It is possible that the effects of this are reflected in the disproportionate numbers of children under-achieving in school and the consequent exclusions.

Geddes (1999), an educational therapist, conducted a study of boys to investigate links between various factors affecting children's behaviour and learning in school. The outcome of this investigation was to identify links between attachment experience and the learning tasks with implications for attachment. Utilizing attachment theory classifications of attachment behaviour, 30 of the children were identified with behaviour which suggested insecure/avoidant attachment. This stems from an early interaction with a primary carer who may have avoided close physical contact in response to the child's anxieties and is experienced as being unavailable and rejecting. The result is the development of an Internal Working Model reflecting low self esteem, poor expectations and mistrust of adults. This was reflected in the responses in the learning situation where the children avoided help from the teacher and focused on the task. This was interpreted as finding the task a safer area in which to engage which was preferred to forming a relationship with the teacher, but they were not always able to perform the task successfully.

An important characteristic of the children with the insecure/avoidant pattern of behaviour was the high incidence of separation, loss and deaths in the families, from which fathers were often missing. This suggested a link between the boys' emotional and behavioural difficulties in school. There was a tendency for these children to be excluded from school and home and entering the care system, and some the criminal justice system. There is a need for teachers to be aware of those children who exhibit difficulty with endings of the school days, terms or years, and the loss of classmates and teachers. Their behaviour may give clues to loss in the families which they have not been helped to process and which may be one of the main factors causing their unsatisfactory behaviour and poor achievement.

Initiatives which aimed to raise the achievement of black pupils in schools were set out in *Aiming High: Raising the Achievement of Minority Ethnic Pupils* (Department for Education and Skills 2003). The framework was built on existing research that shows pupils achieve high educational standards in schools with strong leadership and a culture of high expectation from teachers and pupils to succeed. In these schools there is an ethos of respect with a clear approach to dealing with racism and bad behaviour and effective teaching and learning strategies. Parents and the community are positively encouraged to play a full part in the life and development of the school.

Questions which need to be asked are: why do many children of African Caribbean origin behave in school in ways that warrant exclusion? Why are teachers unable to hold these children? What are the relationships between parents and the school? Are all the ways of helping to understand children's behaviour explored before exclusion is decided upon? Is full use made of educational therapists who are able to work with these children individually? Why are more therapists not assisted to obtain training?

CHILD CARE

Economic and social conditions for many African Caribbean families have improved since the days of the first and second generations of those who came as immigrants. For some there is better housing which enables them to assist in the caring of their grandchildren, and Kinship Care (being cared for by people outside of extended family, such as godparents or close friends of the family) is being looked at more favourably by the care services as an option for parents in need of care facilities for their young children. Some are also able to offer care as foster parents.

Government provision of child care centres and Sure Start programmes, with age- and development-appropriate activities, consistent routines, practice of communication skills, and interaction with peers and adults, helps to reduce some of the challenging behaviour of which young children are capable. Some parents, single or in partnership, choose to pay for private day care in the growing number of play groups and nurseries; yet there are numbers of children in need of care from the local authorities or voluntary services. Some of these are children of young unemployed mothers who lack the support of the fathers of the children. Many of the latter are themselves unemployed and are unable to provide financial support which would ensure housing and other physical needs, and also feel unable to offer emotional support.

Parenting education aims to help parents understand the developmental stages of children and how to care for their children in ways which promote satisfying relationships with them. The parents are helped to understand children's behaviours and to deal with what they consider 'bad behaviour' through courses, with glossy attractive literature. Parenting education also features in the mass media. The main advantage of this increase of information is that there is more discussion about what helps parents to provide secure homes in order to meet the physical, emotional, social and spiritual needs of the children. There are some parents (as I have learned in conversation with them) who think that the information is presented mainly for middle-class families and they cite the practice of putting the child on 'the naughty step' when the housing of some parents prevents them from trying that strategy.

Some unemployed parents are not happy that the government is encouraging them to go out to work and leave their young children in day nurseries when they are being 'taught' that secure relationships between them and their children are formed in the early years of their children's lives. Care in day nurseries is an ongoing debate among developmental psychologists but there are some where the managing staff are aware of the need for consistency of care by sensitive carers.

There were a number of circumstances which necessitated the entry of African Caribbean children into the care system several decades ago, some of which have not changed, such as behaviour and school-related problems, and abandonment of mixed heritage children of Anglo Caribbean mothers (Stone 1983). Reasons now include physical or mental illness of parents, neglect, physical, sexual or emotional abuse, parent's addiction to alcohol or drugs, parents being victims of domestic violence, and parents suffering from HIV/Aids. These circumstances exist within families of all ethnicities but there are disproportionate numbers of African Caribbean children who are looked after in foster care or in residential units. A significant change has been the recruitment of black and other ethnic minority foster carers and the establishment of some black-run residential homes. Just as black professionals reacted to the education system and provided Saturday Schools, so too 'black professionals, social workers and others who worked with children felt keenly that, if they could not prevent children going into care, they needed to be involved in providing the type of cultural environment necessary for the child's development' (Bushell 1992, p.13).

As in earlier times not all of the residential staff are qualified or possess in-depth knowledge of child development, but some of the homes organize in-service training and send their staff on NVQ training. Specialist staff such as psychotherapists, psychologists and psychiatrists are engaged when necessary.

ADOPTION AND FOSTER CARE

In earlier decades, children born of unions between white women and black men were the largest group of children in residential care. They were mainly the offspring of white mothers and black fathers and were labelled 'hard to place'. Today mixed heritage children still make up the largest group of children needing permanent families, and child care practice has become more focused on trying to meet children's need for a racial identity so they are placed in families which reflect their heritage wherever possible.

As in the 1980s and 1990s there is continuing debate about the length of time young children remain in the care of the local authorities, extolling the advantages of permanence through adoption. The debate is ongoing as to whether children should be left waiting for long periods for a family of similar racial/cultural background to be found, rather than placing the child in a white family. In the past, some black children of two black parents have been cared for by white adoptive parents but, while relating their experiences in later life, have revealed the distress of not feeling that they really belonged, or of concealing from their parents the racial discrimination which they suffered outside of the family as in the following case study from my caseload when I practised as a counsellor:

> Ruth, a 21-year-old relating her experiences, claimed that, when at school, she felt ashamed knowing that her black parents had 'given' her away. She dreaded her white adoptive parents visiting the school and in secondary school told her peers that she was fostered. It was only in a therapeutic situation that she spoke of these resentments, hurt, shame and sense of the loss of her 'real self'.

The adults engaged in placing children for adoption thought that being in a family was in their best interest and the adoptive parents also felt committed to caring, but seldom were the special emotional needs of these children considered or their need to look like their parents and to feel that they really belonged to them.

I share the view of Bagley and Young (1982, p.93) that 'The fundamental question to be asked concerns not the most appropriate way in which black children can be adopted, but how to prevent black children being separated from their mothers and coming to the state.' Sometimes it is in the child's best interest if the mother's health is impaired or her lifestyle makes it dangerous, but every effort should be made to explore whether Kinship Care is available, especially when the child has some form of attachment with his or her extended family.

Whereas in the past all connections with the birth family were severed, today adoptive parents are encouraged to allow contact with the child's family, even if only through the exchange of letters and photographs.

There has been active recruitment of black foster carers but sometimes it seems that a great deal of hope was invested in these carers and there was an element of surprise if the racial match did not work and there was a breakdown in the placements. This demonstrated that race is not a qualification. It may well be that some of the foster carers who themselves had experienced attachment and loss and did not have the opportunity to process some of their feelings, may have had them revived by the child or young person in their care. Some agencies have included attachment theory in their training programmes for foster carers and this needs to be done in depth to be beneficial to the carers and the children. Where children have had numerous moves they become in danger of losing opportunities to become attached to a caring adult and may end up feeling completely detached and unable to trust anyone. These are the hapless individuals who may find themselves unable to make and sustain relationships and so become isolated in the society in which they live or may in later life enter the psychiatric system, or be so angry that they act out their aggression and get into conflict with the law and ultimately enter the corrective services.

ADOLESCENTS

Some adolescents, like their peers of other ethnic groups, may engage in behaviour considered delinquent and be referred to the social services with the hope that professional help may effect a change of behaviour. Sometimes this is successful when:

- the social worker is able to work in partnership with the parent/family
- the social worker has knowledge of the effects of early experiences of attachment
- the family understands and accepts the need for the questions which are asked
- the social worker has adequate knowledge of adolescent development and is able to explain this to the family if they seem unaware of some aspects of this
- the social worker has the ability to interview in depth in order to make a comprehensive assessment
- the social worker recognizes when therapeutic help is needed and knows the suitable service for referral.

When young people of African Caribbean origin are referred for assessments, some white workers apply a cultural explanation. The following example from my training experience is a striking example. This case study was presented to a trainee group of white English social workers:

Sarah, 14 years old, was referred for an assessment for persistent truancy from school. When she attended she was disruptive, talked incessantly, interrupted the teacher, refused to pay attention to any instructions and encouraged her peers to join in her escapades. Her parents had admitted that they were unable to control her at home and were worried about her influence on younger siblings.

Sarah was described as of white English origin and trainees were asked to give three initial reactions to the problem presenting. The replies were:

'An adolescent asserting her independence.'

'Wanting to assert her bid for leadership in her peer group.'

'Spoilt by parents.'

Repeating the exercise, the same trainees were asked what their reactions would be if Sarah were of African Caribbean origin:

'Hmm, trouble!'

'Perhaps parents were too strict.'

'No father in the home.'

'Resenting the responsibility of looking after younger siblings.'

When the trainees were asked to analyse their reactions to the two scenarios and their responses, they were surprised that they had not thought about the developmental attributes of adolescence in relation to the black girl. They admitted that they had tried to recall what they had 'learnt' about the cultural and child-rearing practices of African Caribbean families and did not take into account her age or stage of development. They considered the exercise useful in helping them to think holistically about individuals and to recognize what behaviours can be attributed to human growth and development, and how people from different cultural backgrounds demonstrate certain emotions in different ways. For example, to express grief some people cry and wail loudly in public, while others cry silently in private.

The difference in the way that African Caribbean adolescents express emotion may stem from their experiences of racism – a damaged sense of belonging which perhaps contributes to some giving their allegiance to gangs or, in the search for comfort and love, girls entering into relationships with members of the opposite sex too readily and becoming pregnant.

This is not to imply that some social workers from African Caribbean backgrounds who are British born and bred, and who have internalized the British culture, will not possess an approach to their clients similar to that of their white colleagues, based on their social work training. All workers need to guard against the tendency to make assumptions based on insufficient knowledge of the client group with whom they work.

PARENTS' ATTEMPTS TO GIVE CHILDREN A SENSE OF BELONGING TO THEIR ORIGINAL CULTURE

Some parents took their children born in Britain back to Caribbean countries in order for them to experience the cultural background in which they (the parents) had been reared. Some of the children loved the freedom of the rural areas, the sun and the sea. Older ones, though, often found themselves uncomfortable in the new environment, not sharing their parents' sense of belonging to the Caribbean.

For example, in conversation with a group of adolescent girls aged 16–17 they described visiting the Caribbean in their early teens and they were unanimous in feeling strangers there. They spoke differently. They disliked the food, did not understand the 'Creole' language and were themselves not always understood. After a short time in the Caribbean they longed for 'home'. Though eager to return to London, despite the fact that in London they are frequently subjected to verbal racist abuse and asked, 'Why don't you go back where you came from?'

In this way little has changed from the time of the first-generation migrants: one of them, reminiscing, claimed that he had lived in Britain for over 60 years, saw active service in the RAF during the war, was successful in his career, but yet lacked any real sense of identity and belonging. When young people are treated as though they do not belong either in Britain or the Caribbean it is painful and confusing, and undermines their sense of identity. Little wonder that some children drift into becoming disaffected youths who need the attention of the caring professions.

Currently, there is still debate in social work circles about the extent to which culture should be considered as being relevant when working with families from black and other minorities. There are some white professionals working with black clients who admit to anxieties about 'being called racist' if they enquire about cultural practices. Sometimes these fears and anxieties may be so great that the workers become ineffective in making accurate assessments. The need for training in intercultural social work has been recognized. Training should enable workers to maintain a balance between, on the one hand, being aware of shared and universal human characteristics and not attributing the client's problems to some cultural peculiarity and, on the other, not neglecting cultural variability with the aim of treating everyone 'the same'.

There has been a considerable increase in the number of young people cared for by foster carers over the years who have been given a new lease of life. But unfortunately, there are instances where as children they have had numerous moves which have erased any opportunity for becoming attached to a caring adult. They then run the risk of feeling completely detached and unable to trust anyone. These are the hapless individuals who may be found in later life in the psychiatric systems or in conflict with the law and in the corrective services.

Observing the initiatives undertaken over the last decades in the social care field, there is evidence that efforts, at statutory and voluntary levels, have been, and are continuing to be, made to find solutions to some of the problems which contribute to the dysfunction of families within society generally, and within black and minority families in particular. Nevertheless, some African Caribbean families still experience high rates of unemployment, insufficient child care for full-time working mothers, disproportionate numbers of young people in detention centres and in prison, domestic violence and children needing to be looked after. More recently there are grave concerns among families and professionals in the social care system and in the judicial systems about the high rates of violence, knife and gun crimes in the country, in which numbers of black youths are involved in fatal incidences. There are also concerns about children being excluded from schools, high rates of teenage pregnancy, and high incidence of mental disorder.

It is worth bearing in mind that not all aspects of cultural practices of child-rearing in majority and minority ethnic groups are conducive to children's well-being, and some are even detrimental to their physical and emotional health, for example, sending children to bed without a meal, or severe corporal punishment of children with inappropriate instruments such as the buckle end of a belt, or electric flex. Some parents of various cultural backgrounds believe in instilling discipline in their children through administering corporal punishment. African Caribbean parents are often heard to say that their parents were strict and disciplined them by 'beating' them and 'it did them no harm'. Further conversations reveal that often parents did not explain or discuss reasons for the corporal punishment and this left them as children feeling aggrieved and resentful and harbouring the feeling that they were unfairly treated. Others who described a close relationship with parents claimed that if they were beaten, they must have deserved it and they tried hard not to repeat the behaviour which displeased their parents.

An added dimension which sometimes prevents those in the helping professions from acknowledging that basic human needs are similar is attitudes towards people of a different race and ethnicity. The words of Jafar Kareem (2000, p.20) are pertinent in this respect: 'In accepting and working with differences in human beings, however, one must try to seek the very universality that exists in diversity.'

As mentioned above, many white professionals working with black clients admit to anxieties about 'being called racist'. Sometimes these fears and anxieties may be so great that the workers become ineffective in making appropriate decisions in the interest of the children with whom they work. Workers need to be conscious of their attitudes, and of the different belief systems of people that are of a different ethnic background to themselves with whom they work. Workers also need to be aware of when the specific problems of clients are exacerbated by unexpressed grief and mourning, which may come from separation and traumatic events in their early lives which they have never been able to disclose to anyone. When disadvantaged families seek help after traumatic events in their lives, those in the helping professions can empower them by giving them time to tell their narratives, and encouraging them to reflect on how their past experiences may still be influencing their feelings and reactions in the present situation.

CASE STUDY

Some reactions of individuals who have experienced disturbances of attachment to significant figures may be of a psychosomatic nature and if they are unfamiliar with therapeutic services they may frequent the surgeries of general practitioners. The following case study illustrates how familiarity with the principles of attachment theory and knowledge of the client's migration history helped an African Caribbean client in the resolution of some of her problems.

Linda, aged 42 years, of African Caribbean origin, had been referred for therapeutic help as she complained of being depressed. She had been seeing her general practitioner, but had refused to take the medication he prescribed for fear of becoming addicted. Because of her indisposition she had not been performing effectively at her place at work and was reprimanded by her manager in the presence of younger colleagues. Linda thought this was discriminatory. She obtained sick leave from her doctor but at the end of the period she decided to resign her job. Linda explained that she felt the office was no longer a safe place and she was traumatized, not only by the loss of employment but also by the loss of her prestige.

The main theme that emerged from Linda's narrative was the numerous losses which she experienced from early childhood, during adolescence, and adulthood. She had been left by her parents when she was two years old with her grandmother who idolized her and whom she loved and missed all her life after she came to live in England. Her relationship with her mother was never close, but she related fairly well with her father and her brother and sister. She had entered into relations with a partner, but she was never able to trust him nor to feel that she was loved, so she repeatedly tested him until he became impatient with her behaviour, and eventually he terminated the relationship.

Bearing Linda's immigration history in mind, it was decided that work needed to be done to help Linda to mourn her losses and to try to come to accept what had happened, which involved dealing both with anger and with feelings of despair, before moving on to dealing with changed circumstances. This work would be based on attachment theory.

Bowlby (1988) identified five tasks which guided work of this nature:

1. The provision of a secure base from which the client would be able to explore past painful experiences.

2. Helping the client to consider how he or she engaged in relationships with significant attachment figures and what the client's expectations and behaviour were.

3. Encouragement of the client to examine the relationship with the therapist/social worker and the way that he or she is thought of as an attachment figure.

4. Helping the client to think about how childhood and adolescent experiences, particularly in relation to parents, influence the

present. This task is often painful and it may be hard to express feelings or ideas about parents which previously seemed unthinkable.

5. Helping the client to understand that images of self and of others which may have been derived from life experiences or from parents may not be appropriate for the present nor for the future.

Linda was insightful and responded well. Upon reflection she was able to make the link with the feelings of anger she had repressed all through her life, especially with her mother, and she saw that this had been displaced onto her manager who had behaved in a similar way to how her mother had often behaved in the presence of her siblings.

OLDER PEOPLE

The first generation of immigrants as described in Chapter 2 are now elderly. Some have fulfilled their dream of returning to their home countries which has again broken the family attachments, but because of increased air travel and easier means of communication contact for those who want it is possible. Some of them are great-grandmothers and return to visit their families.

Many have reconciled themselves to the fact that their old age in Britain will be different from that in their home countries. The extended family pattern is uncommon and a high proportion of them live alone. Their children may have moved to different cities for employment reasons or to live in the area of their partner, and some have gone abroad for business purposes. Those whose children live nearby cannot always guarantee support from them because of the earlier relationship patterns and conflict which they have not been able to resolve, and sometimes relationships have not been formed with those who were born in Britain due to a clash of cultures, so some are very isolated. In the earlier years homes for older people did not cater for the needs of old black and ethic minority people and so when residential care was necessary, there was reluctance on the part of older people to accept it. There are now homes run by people of their own ethnic group who can cater to their taste in food and activities and engage them in reminiscence work, but not nearly in sufficient numbers to meet the demand, and there are still some families who retain the values of caring for their elderly parents. It would be useful for these people to receive necessary help for them to do so. In this time of cutting back benefits this may not be possible.

Many older people who enjoy good health are active in the help they provide for caring for their grandchildren and even before the cutbacks by government, grandparenting voluntary organisations have been campaigning for Kinship Care to be supported.

Religion plays an important part in the lives of some older people. Many of them have found comfort in black-led churches which not only meet their spiritual needs, but also provide friendships and a sense of belonging, as well as meeting material needs such as providing meals, transport, social activities and visiting when ill. In 1982 Vivienne Coombe, a social worker, stated that work with older minorities was a new and exciting field which enabled social workers to utilize a variety of social work techniques. This includes individual work with older persons, in which they are encouraged to talk about their past and so process their feelings of loss of their youth, families, work and sometimes their health. Other techniques are in group work and work in the community, tapping resources of individual volunteers and voluntary groups who may be useful in relieving the isolation which besets so many older people. Much will depend on the older person's earlier experiences of making and sustaining relationships and that of the worker as well. Careful selection of workers needs to be made and appropriate training for work with older people given.

There are some young adults who bemoan the fact that their grandparents never communicated much with them about their places of origin and even now are reluctant to do so. It may be that the memories were too painful, especially of their migration experiences and those of racism and disadvantage in their early lives in the country.

CONCLUSION

In this book a snapshot of the origins of African Caribbean families was given in order to place the families in context and to give an indication of the Caribbean culture and child-rearing practices. Some of the problems which were faced through separation and reunion of some African Caribbean families, as explained by mothers and by women who were separated as children, were described. The samples for my research were small but the studies illustrated the pattern of the separation and reunion which affected the lives of the immigrant families. Subsequently talking to hundreds of women who had similar experiences confirmed my findings.

In contemporary society it seems that many of the African Caribbean people born in Britain have internalized the British culture and do not share the feelings of belonging to the countries of their parents and grandparents.

Sudarkasa (1970) named four cultural values which underpinned African life: (1) respect, (2) responsibility, (3) restraint and (4) reciprocity. He claimed that these had been inherited by families of African origin in the diaspora. These had been eroded and replaced with what could be considered pillars of the nuclear family: (1) individualism, (2) isolation and (3) self sufficiency, which have undermined black families everywhere and left the poorest exposed and vulnerable. This last has some resonance in some African Caribbean families in Britain today.

Placing the studies in the theoretical context of attachment theory I support the notion as propounded by Bowlby that experiences in the early life of the child influence later relationships (Bowlby 1979).

Very often in work with clients who have had experiences of separation and loss, little or scant attention has been paid to the impact of the disruption of the attachment relationships which often adversely affect the emotional and physical health of the individual. If social workers are prepared to utilize their knowledge of attachment theory, in their capacities as key workers, and spend time encouraging individuals to tell and reflect upon their narratives, very often clients are able to make links with their early experiences and their present feelings. This is a first step in the process of healing. Sometimes a client may need a longer time spent than the social worker is able to give; referral to an appropriate service needs to be made. This may be to an individual therapist whose training is orientated in attachment theory. Some clients may also benefit by attending a support group led by someone with knowledge of the theory, where the clients may benefit by sharing their experiences and hearing the experiences of others and the strategies they employed to help them to move on to a more comfortable stage.

The value of utilizing the principles of attachment theory, separation and loss in working with Caribbean families across the age range would appear to be considerable and necessary in order to remove the assumptions that problems are mainly the result of the family structures or are innate in their cultural practices.

Policy makers need also to be convinced that working with clients in depth and in a painstaking way is cost effective and workers should be given the training and the time and employed in sufficient numbers in order that their work (with realistic numbers of clients) will be more liable to produce positive outcomes. Currently in the days of recession an increase of staff and additional money spent in training may not be possible, but it is hoped that it will be borne in mind when the recession is over. In Bowlby's early studies he stated his belief that the cause of unhappiness, psychiatric illnesses and delinquency could be attributed to loss and he believed that in working with individuals this was often missed (Bowlby 1965). I am of the opinion that today the same may still be true.

The studies used here have raised many questions and highlighted several which may be usefully researched among African Caribbean families. There are several areas to research:

- the involvement of fathers in child-rearing in the British context and patterns of child–father attachments

- the impact on children born in England when siblings from the Caribbean joined the family

- parents' reasons for requesting children to be 'looked after' and their involvement with the children during care and when they leave care

- older African Caribbean residents in institutional care in Britain

- single mature women of African Caribbean origin and their willingness to adopt.

There is also room for comparative studies with other groups within society, such as families from some West African countries who separate from their children through leaving them in boarding schools to complete their secondary education, before joining them in Britain. How do they cope with the reunions?

This is by no means an exhaustive list of research topics. In this multicultural society and with a growing population of people suffering from separation and loss, psychotherapists, psychologists, social workers and teachers could all usefully consider the effectiveness of utilizing attachment theory in their work with those whose attachments have been broken, not only in childhood for, as Bowlby emphasized, the theory is relevant from the cradle to the grave.

Appendix I

Map of the Caribbean

The map on the following page shows the islands that comprise the Caribbean, the history of which is described in Chapter 1.

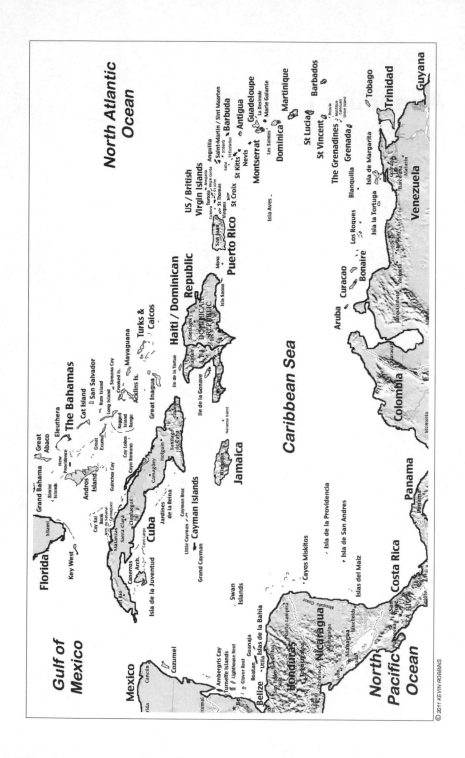

Appendix 2

Revised Separation Reunion

Interview Schedule (SRIS)

Initials: _____

Age: _____

Civil status: _____

Number of children: _____ Ages of children: _____

Occupation: _____

PRE-MIGRATION

1. How old were you when left in the Caribbean? Alone or with brothers and sisters?

2. With whom were you left?

3. Who took care of you?

4. Did you think your carer was your mother?

5. What did you call her?

6. What were you told about your mother?

7. What memories have you of your feelings about mother not being there?

8. What did you as a small child remember asking about your mother?

9. What were you told about your mother?

10. What did you think about your mother leaving you?

11. How old were you when you were told that you were leaving to join your mother in England and what did you feel about it?

12. Did you want to leave the Caribbean to travel to England to live with your mother?

13. What did you think that it would be like living with your mother?

14. Why did you think your mother left you?

15. What did you think it would be like living with your mother?

16. How did you feel when you were told you were leaving to come to England?

17. What preparation had you for leaving the West Indies to come to England?

18. What did your carer tell you why you were leaving her?

19. How did you feel about her allowing you to leave?

20. How do you think she felt about you leaving her?

21. What did you look forward to when you knew you were coming to England?

22. How did you feel about leaving the West Indies; family, friends, the country?

23. Who accompanied you on the journey?

IMMIGRATION

24. How did you feel when you arrived?

25. Did you recognize your mother? Father? If yes, how did you feel? If no?

26. How do you think your mother felt at seeing you?

POST-MIGRATION

27. How did you feel when you saw your brothers and sisters who were born in England?

28. How did you think they felt at seeing you?

29. What did you recall about life in the West Indies and to whom did you talk about those left behind?

30. What did you miss about West Indies?

31. What did you like about joining the family?

32. What did you not like?

33. How did you think the family felt about you joining them?

34. How did you get on at school, with peers and teachers?

35. How easy/difficult was it for you to make friends?

36. What did you and children who had similar experiences recall about the West Indies when you lived there?

37. How did you feel when in school and how did you progress?

38. What were your qualifications when you left school?

39. Were you encouraged by your mother/father to further your studies?

40. Did you want to study further or to go to work?

41. How easy or difficult was it for you to be employed?

42. How easy or difficult was it for you to build relationships with colleagues at work?

43. How old were you when you left home? Under what circumstances?

44. What were your feelings when you left home?

45. How do you think your mother felt? And the rest of your family?

46. What contact did you maintain with your mother/parents after leaving home?

47. With whom did you live after leaving home?

48. If with a partner, how did you relate to each other?

49. How similar/different was your partner's experience of early childhood to yours?

50. What did you share and discuss of your experiences?

51. How helpful or unhelpful was having a partner of similar background to you?

52. What do you feel about who cares for young children in early childhood?

53. What effect do you think it has on the child to be cared for by someone who is not the mother?

54. What effect does reuniting have on child and mother?

55. Which experiences of your early childhood do you think have influenced who you are today?

56. What connections, if any, do you make with your early experience and your depressive feelings?

57. How do you cope with separation and loss in your life?

58. How are your moods generally?

59. What triggers your feelings of depression?

60. How easy is it for you to trust others and make and sustain relationships?

References

Ainsworth, M.D.S. (1967) *Infancy in Uganda. Infant Care and the Growth of Love.* Baltimore, MD: Johns Hopkins University Press.

Ainsworth, M.D.S. (1982) 'Attachment: Retrospect and Prospect.' In C.M. Parkes and J. Stevenson-Hinde (eds) *The Place of Attachment in Human Behaviour.* London: Tavistock Publications.

Ainsworth, M.D.S., Blehar, M.C., Waters, E. and Wall, S. (1978) *Patterns of Attachment: A Psychological Study of the Strange Situation.* Hillsdale, NJ: Erlbaum.

Ainsworth, M. and Wittig, B.A. (1969) 'Attachment and the Exploratory Behaviour of One Year Olds in a Strange Situation.' In In B.M. Foss (ed.) *Determinants of Infant Behaviour, Vol. 4.* London: Methuen.

Alexander, Z. and Dewjee, A. (1981) *Roots in Britain: Black and Asian Citizens from Elizabeth I to Elizabeth II.* London: Brent Library Services.

Arnold, E. (2000) 'Intercultural social work.' In J. Kareem and R. Littlewood (eds) *Intercultural Therapy.* Second Edition. Oxford: Blackwell Science.

Arnold, E. (2001) 'Broken attachments of women from the West Indies separated from mothers in early childhood.' Unpublished PhD Thesis, University of London.

Arnold, E. and Geddes, H. (2004) 'Issues of attachment, separation and loss through immigration of Afro-Caribbean families to the United Kingdom.' *Young Minds Newsletter,* July, 1–2.

Bagley, C. and Young, L. (1982) 'Policy Dilemmas and the Adoption of Black Children.' In J. Cheetham (ed.) *Social Work and Ethnicity.* London: George Allen & Unwin.

Barrett, H. (2006) *Attachment and the Perils of Parenting.* London: National Family and Parenting Institute.

Beckles, H.McD. and Shepherd, V.A. (2004) *Liberties Lost: Caribbean Indigenous Societies and Slave Systems.* Cambridge: Cambridge University Press.

Benjamin, F. (1998) *Coming to England.* London: Puffin Books.

Berthoud, R. (2000) *Family Formation in Multicultural Britain: Three Patterns of Diversity.* Essex: Institute for Social and Economic Research.

Blake, J. (1961) *Family Structure in Jamaica.* New York: Glencoe Press.

Bonham-Carter, M. (1987) 'The liberal hour and race relations law.' *Journal of Ethnic and Migration Studies 14,* 1–2, 1–8.

Bousquet, B. and Douglas, C. (1991) *West Indian Women At War: British Racism in World War II.* London: Lawrence & Wishart.

Bowlby, J. (1940) 'Psychological aspects.' In R. Padley and M. Cole (eds) *Evacuation Survey: A Report to the Fabian Society.* London: Routledge.

Bowlby, J. (1944) 'Forty-four juvenile thieves, their character and home life.' *International Journal of Psychoanalysis 25,* 1–57.

Bowlby, J. (1952) *Maternal Care and Mental Health.* Geneva: World Health Organisation.

Bowlby, J. (1965) *Child Care and the Growth of Love.* Second Edition. London: Penguin.

Bowlby, J. (1973) *Attachment and Loss. Vol 2: Separation, Anxiety and Anger.* London: Hogarth Press.

Bowlby, J. (1979) *The Making and Breaking of Affectional Bonds.* London: Tavistock.

Bowlby, J. (1980) *Attachment and Loss. Vol 3: Sadness and Depression.* London and New York: Hogarth Press.

Bowlby, J. (1982a) *Attachment and Loss. Vol 1: Attachment.* Second Edition. London: Hogarth Press and the Institute of Psychoanalysis.

Bowlby, J. (1982b) 'Attachment and loss: retrospect and prospect.' *American Journal of Orthopsychiatry 52,* 664–678.

Bowlby, J. (1988) *A Secure Base: Clinical Applications of Attachment Theory.* London: Routledge.

Bowlby, J. (1991) 'Postscript.' In C.M. Parkes, J. Stevenson-Hinde and P. Marris (eds) *Attachment Across the Life Cycle.* London: Routledge.

Bowlby, R. (2004) *Fifty Years of Attachment Theory: The Donald Winnicott Memorial Lectures.* London: Karnac Books.

Bowlby, J. and Robertson, J. (1956) 'A Two-Year-Old Goes to Hospital.' In K. Soddy (ed.) *Mental Health and Infant Development, Vol 1: Papers and Discussion.* London: Routledge and Kegan Paul.

Braithwaite, L. (1959) 'Social and economic change in the Caribbean.' In *Children of the Caribbean – Their Mental Health Needs: Proceedings of the Second Caribbean Conference for Mental Health.* St Thomas Virgin Islands, Department of Extra-Mural Studies, University of the West Indies.

Braithwaite, E. (1970) *Folk Culture of the Slaves in Jamaica.* London: New Beacon Books.

Braithwaite, E. (1971) *The Development of a Creole Society in Jamaica, 1770–1820.* Oxford: Oxford University Press.

Brody, E.B. (1981) *Sex, Contraception and Motherhood in Jamaica.* Cambridge, MA and London: Harvard University Press.

Brown, J., Newland, A., Anderson, P. and Chevannes, B. (1997) 'Caribbean Fatherhood: Under-researched, Misunderstood.' In J.L. Roopnarine and J. Brown (eds) *Caribbean Families: Diversity Among Ethnic Groups.* Greenwich, CT: Ablex Publishing Corporation.

Bryan, B., Dadzie, S. and Scafe, S. (1985) *The Heart of the Race: Black Women's Lives in Britain.* London: Virago Press.

Burke, A.W. (1974) 'Mental illness and psychiatric treatment in relation to immigrants.' Unpublished paper delivered to the Intercultural Group, British Association of Social Workers (BASW), Birmingham.

Bushell, W. (1992) *Black Children in Care. Report To Ethnic Study Group.* London.

Cassidy, J. (1988) 'The self as related to child–mother attachment.' *Child Development 59,* 121–131.

Clarke, E. (1966) *My Mother who Fathered Me.* Second Edition. London: Unwin.

Coard, B. (1971) *How the West Indian Child is made Educationally Subnormal by the British School System.* London: New Beacon Books.

Comitas, L. and Lowenthal, D. (1973) *Work and Family Life: A West Indian Perspective.* New York: Anchor Press Doubleday.

Commission For Racial Equality (2006) *Housing in Terror.* London: CRE.

Coombe, V. (1982) 'Social Work with Ethnic Minority Elderly People.' In J. Cheetham (ed.) *Social Work and Ethnicity.* London. George Allen & Unwin.

Crawford-Brown, C. (1997) 'The Impact of Parent–Child Socialisation on the Development of Conduct Disorder in Jamaican Male Adolescents.' In J.L. Roopnarine and J. Browne (eds) *Caribbean Families: Diversity among Ethnic Groups.* Greenwich, CT: Ablex Publishing Corporation.

Crittenden, P.M. (1985) 'Maltreated infants: Vulnerability and resilience.' *Journal of Child Psychology and Psychiatry 26*, 85–96.

Davies, R. (2010) 'The 50th Anniversary of the Platt Report: From Exclusion to Toleration to Parental Participation in the Care of the Hospitalised Child.' *Journal of Child Care* 14, 1, 16–23.

Davison B. (1962) *Black Mother Africa*. London: Gollancz.

Department for Children, Schools and Families (DCSF) (2009) *Statistics on Permanent and Fixed Period Exclusions from Schools and Exclusion Appeals in England 2007–2008*. London: DCSF.

Department for Communities and Local Governments (2008) *Housing in England 2007–08*. London: The Stationery Office.

Department for Education and Skills (2003) *Aiming High: Raising the Achievement of Minority Ethnic Pupils*. London: Department for Education and Skills.

Dookhan, I. (1971) *A Pre-Emancipation History of the West Indies*. London: Collins.

Ellis, P. (ed.) (1986) *Women of the Caribbean*. London and Atlantic Highlands, NJ: Zed Books.

Erikson, E.H. (1963) *Childhood and Society*. New York: Norton.

Fitzherbert, K. (1967) *West Indian Children in London*. London: Bell and Sons.

Frazier, F. (1953) 'The negro family in the United States.' *British Journal of Sociology 4*, 293–313.

Freud, A. and Burlingham, D.T. (1973) *Infants Without Families: Reports on the Hampstead Nurseries, 1939–1945*. New York: International Universities Press.

Forde, N.M. (1981) *Women and the Law*. Barbados: University of the West Indies.

Garner, R. (2010) 'Social workers were "enthusiastic removers of children".' *The Independent*, 13 April.

Geddes, H. (1999) 'Attachment, behaviour and learning: implications for the teacher, the pupil and the task.' *Journal of Educational Therapy and Therapeutic Teaching 8*, 1–34.

Gillian, R. (1997) 'Beyond permanence? The importance of resilience in child placement practice and planning.' *Adoption and Fostering Quarterly Journal 21*, 1, 14–15.

Glass, R. (1960) *The Newcomers*. London: Allen and Unwin.

Gorell Barnes, G. (1975) 'Seen but not heard: The isolated West Indian parent and child in London.' *Social Work Today 5*, 646–648.

Gorell Barnes, G. (1977) 'Family and Group Work with West Indian Clients.' In *Studies in Inter-Cultural Social Work*. Birmingham: BASW.

Gorell Barnes, G., Thompson, P., Daniel, G. and Burchardt, N. (1997) *Growing up in Stepfamilies*. London: Oxford University Press.

Goring, B. (2004) 'The perspectives of UK Caribbean parents on schooling and education: Change and continuity.' Unpublished PhD Thesis. London, South Bank University.

Green, V. (1973) 'Methodological Problems Involved in the Study of the Urban Family.' in E. Gerber (ed.) *The Family in the Caribbean: Proceedings of the Second Conference on the Family in the Caribbean*. Rio Piedras: University of Puerto Rico Press.

Harlow, H.F. and Zimmerman, R.R. (1959) 'Affectional responses of the infant monkey.' *Science 130*, 421–426.

Hawkes, B. (2008) 'The Gun Crisis in the Black Community: A Legacy of Loss, Separation and Broken Attachments?' In E. Arnold and B. Hawkes (eds) *Internalising the Historical Past: Issues For Separation and Moving On*. Newcastle: Cambridge Scholars Publishing.

Hearne, J. and Nettleford, R. (1963) *Public Affairs in Jamaica No 1: Our Heritage*. Jamaica: The Department of Extra-Mural Studies, University of the West Indies.

Henriques, F. (1953) *Family and Colour in Jamaica*. London: Gibbon and Kee.

Henriques, F. (1973) 'West Indian Family Organization.' In L. Comitas and D. Lowenthal (eds) *Work and Family Life: West Indian Perspectives*. New York: Anchor Books.

Herman, J.L. (1992) Trauma and Recovery. New York: Basic.

Herskovits, M.J. (1966) 'The New World Negro.' In F.S. Herskovits (ed.) *Selected Papers in Afro-American Studies*. Indiana: Indiana University Press.

Hill, C.S. (1963) *West Indian Migrants and The London Churches*. London: Institute of Race Relations, Oxford University Press.

Hinde, R.A. (1965) Rhesus Monkey Aunts.' In Foss, B.M. (ed.) *Determinants of Infant Behaviour, Vol. 3*. London: Methuen and New York: Wiley.

Hogan, M.G. (ed.) (2001) *The Oxford Book of Spirituals*. London: Oxford University Press.

Hogg, P. (1979) *Slavery: The Afro-American Experience*. London: The British Library.

Holmes, J. (1993) *John Bowlby and Attachment Theory*. London: Routledge.

Holmes, J. (1994) 'Attachment theory: A secure theoretical base for counselling.' *Psychodynamic Counselling 11*, October, 65–78.

Holmes, J. (1998) Psychodynamics, narrative and "intentional causality".' *British Journal of Psychiatry 173*, 279–282.

Hood, C., Oppe, T.E., Pless, I.B. and Apte, E. (1970) *Children of West Indian Immigrants*. London: The Institute of Race Relations.

Jones, A., Sharpe, J. and Sogren, M. (2004) *Children of Migration: A Study of the Care Management and Psycho-social Status of Children of Parents who Migrated*. University of the West Indies, St. Augustine, Trinidad, West Indies.

Kareem, J. (2000) 'The Nafsiyat Intercultural Therapy Centre: Ideas and Experience in Intercultural Therapy.' In J. Kareem and R. Littlewood (eds) *Intercultural Therapy: Themes, Interpretations and Practice*. Second Edition. Oxford: Blackwell.

Kareem, J. and Littlewood, R. (eds) (2000) *Intercultural Therapy: Themes, Interpretations and Practice*. Second Edition. Oxford: Blackwell.

Klein, M. (1975) *The Psychoanalysis of Children*. (Translation by A. Strachey.) New York: Dell Publishing.

Littlewood, R. (1986) 'Ethnic Minorities and the Mental Health Act: Patterns of Explanation.' *Bulletin of the Royal College of Psychiatrists 10*, 306–308.

Littlewood, R. (1993) 'Ideology, Camouflage or Contingency? Racism in British Society.' *Transcultural Psychiatry 30*, 3, 243–290.

Littlewood, R. (2000) 'Towards an Intercultural Therapy.' In J. Kareem and R. Littlewood (eds) *Intercultural Therapy: Themes, Interpretations and Practice*. Second Edition. Oxford: Blackwell.

Lloyd, A.J. and Robertson, E. (1971) *Social Welfare in Trindad and Tobago*. Trinidad: Antilles Research Associates.

Lorenz, K. (1951) *Studies in Animal and Human Behaviour*. Oxford: Clarendon Press.

Lowenthal, D. (1972) *West Indian Societies*. London: Oxford University Press.

Main, M., Kaplan, N. and Cassidy, J. (1985) 'Security in Childhood and Adulthood: A Move to the Level of Representation.' In I. Bretherton and E. Waters (eds) *Growing Points of Attachment Theory and Research. Monographs of the Society for Researching Child Development 50*, 1.

Main, M. and Hesse, E. (1990) 'The Insecure disorganized/disoriented attachment pattern in infancy: precursors and sequelae.' In M. Greenberg, D. Cicchetti and E.M. Cummings (eds) *Attachment During the Preschool Years: Theory, Research and Intervention*. Chicago: University of Chicago Press.

Main, M. and Solomon, J. (1990) 'Procedures for Identifying Infants as Disorganized/Disoriented during the Ainsworth Strange Situation.' In M. Greenberg, D. Cicchetti and M. Cummings (eds) *Attachment in the Preschool Years: Theory, Research and Intervention*. Chicago, IL: University of Chicago Press.

Main, M. and Weston, D. (1982) 'Avoidance of the Attachment Figure in Infancy: Descriptions and Interpretations.' In C.M. Parkes and J. Stevenson-Hinde (eds) *The Place of Attachment in Human Behaviour*. New York: Wiley.

Manley, M. (1974) *The Politics of Change: A Jamaican Testament*. London: Andre Deutsch.

Marris, P. (1991) 'The Social Construction of Uncertainty.' In C.M. Parkes, J. Stevenson-Hinde and P. Marris (eds) *Attachment Across the Life Cycle*. London: Routledge.

Massiah, J. (1982) *Women who Head Households: Women in the Caribbean: Project Research Papers*. Barbados: Institute of Social and Economic Research, University of the West Indies.

McPherson, W. (1999) *The McPherson Report*. London: HMSO.

Ministry of Health (1959) *The Welfare of Children in Hospital: Report of a Committee of the Central Health Services Council*. London: HMSO.

Morrish, I. (1971) *The Background of Immigrant Children*. London: George Allen and Unwin Ltd.

Norris, K. (1962) *Jamaica: The Search for Identity*. London: Oxford University Press.

Ojike, M. (1946) *My Africa*. New York: The John Day Company.

Parkes, C.M. (1972) *Bereavement: Studies of Grief in Adult Life*. Harmondsworth and New York: Penguin.

Paton, G. (2007) 'Where White British pupils are in a Minority.' *Telegraph*, 27 September.

Patterson, O. (1967) *The Sociology of Slavery: An Analysis of the Origins, Development and Structure of the Negro Slave Society in Jamaica*. London: Gibbon and Kee.

Patterson, S. (1965) *Dark Strangers*. Harmondsworth: Penguin.

Peach, C. (1968) *West Indian Migration to Britain: A Social Geography*. Oxford: Institute of Race Relations, Oxford University Press.

Pearcy, G.E. (1965) *The West Indian Scene*. New Jersey, NJ: Ian Nostrand.

Peppard, N. (1987) 'The community relations commission: A note on its foundations and role.' *New Community 14*, 1/2.

Peppard, N. (1980) 'Towards effective race relations training.' *New Community 8*, 1 & 2, 99–106.

Prince, M. (1831) *The History of Mary Prince, A West Indian Slave, Related by Herself*. (1987 Edition. Edited by Moira Ferguson.) London: Routledge & Kegan Paul Ltd.

Reynolds, T. (2005) *Caribbean Mothers: Identity and Experience in the UK*. London: The Tufnell Press.

Richardson, D. (1993) 'Mother Knows Best: Theories of Childrearing Since the Second World War.' In D. Richardson (ed.) *Women, Motherhood and Childrearing*. London: Macmillan.

Richmond, A.H. (1961) *The Colour Problem*. London: Penguin.

Riley, D. (1983) *War in the Nursery*. London: Virago.

Roberts, G.W. and Mills, D.O. (1958) 'Report: Study of external migration.' *Social and Economic Studies 7*, 2.

Robertson, E.E. (1975) 'Out of sight – not out of mind. A study of West Indian mothers living in England, separated for long periods from their children through leaving them behind when migrating and subsequently reunited.' Unpublished MPhil Thesis, University of Sussex.

Robertson, J. and Robertson, J. (1973) *Young Children in Brief Separations*. Nacton, Suffolk: Concorde Films Council.

Rose, E.J.B., Deakin, N., Jackson, V., Abrams, M. *et al.* (1969) *Colour and Citizenship. A Report on British Race Relations*. Oxford: Oxford University Press.

Russell-Brown, P.A., Norville, B. and Griffiths, C. (1997) 'Child Shifting: A Survival Strategy for Teenage Mothers.' In J. Roopnarine and J. Brown (eds) *Caribbean Families: Diversity Among Ethnic Groups*. Greenwich, CT: Ablex Publishing Corporation.

Rutter, M. (1981) *Maternal Deprivation Reassessed*. London: Penguin Education.

Rutter, M. and Rutter, M. (1992) *Developing Minds: Challenge and Continuity Across the Life Span*. Harmondsworth: Penguin Books.

Salter, M.D. (1940) *An Evaluation Based Upon the Concept of Security*. University of Toronto Studies Child Development Series no. 18. Toronto: University of Toronto.

Scarman, Lord (1981) *The Scarman Report*. London: HMSO.

Schafer, R. (1999) 'Disappointment and disappointedness.' *The International Journal of Psychoanalysis 80*, 65, 1093–1104.

Sharpe, J. (1997) 'Mental Health Issues and Family Socialization in the Caribbean.' In J. Roopnarine and J. Brown (eds) *Caribbean Families: Diversity Among Ethnic Groups*. Greenwich, CT: Ablex Publishing Corporation.

Sharpe, J. (2001) 'Separation and Loss, Sadness and Survival: A Caribbean Legacy?' In L. Connelly, A. Gaitanidis and L. John-Baptiste (eds) *Legacies of Loss: The Black Child in Focus*. London: Goldsmiths College and Nafsiyat Conference Report.

Shorey-Bryan, N. (1986) 'The Making of Male–Female Relationships in the Caribbean.' In P. Ellis (ed.) *Women of the Caribbean*. London: Zed Books Ltd.

Simey, T. (1946) *Welfare Planning in the West Indies*. Oxford: Clarendon Press.

Smith, M.G. (1962) *West Indian Family Structure*. Seattle: University of Washington Press.

Smith, M.G. (1965) *The Plural Society in the British West Indies*. Berkeley, CA: University of California Press.

Smith, R.T. (1956) *The Negro Family in British Guiana*. London: Routledge and Kegan Paul.

Smith, R.T. (1988) *Kinship and Class in the West Indies: A Genealogical Study of Jamaica and Guyana*. Cambridge: Cambridge University Press.

Starobin, R.S. (ed.) (1974) *Blacks in Bondage*. New York: New Viewpoints.

Stewart-Prince, G.S. (1968) 'Emotional Problems of Children Reunited with their Migrant Families.' In J.P Triseliotis (ed.) *Social Work with Coloured Immigrants and Their Families*. Oxford: Oxford University Press.

Stewart-Prince, G.S. (1972) 'Mental Health Problems in Pre-school West Indian Children.' In J.P. Triseliotis (ed.) *Social Work with Coloured Immigrants and their Families*. London: Oxford University Press.

Stone, M. (1983) *Ethnic Minority Children in Care*. Social Science Research Council. Unpublished.

Sudarkasa, N. (1970) *Black Families*. Newbury Park, CA: Sage Publications.

Thomas, L. (2001) 'The Impact of Separation and Loss on Children Whose Parents were Left Behind.' In L. Connelly, A. Gaitanidis and L. John-Baptiste (eds) *Legacies of Loss: The Black Child in Focus*. London: Goldsmiths College and Nafsiyat Conference Report.

Thomas, L. (2008) 'Reflecting on internalising the historical past.' In E. Arnold and B. Hawkes (eds) *Internalising the Historical Past: Issues for Separation and Moving On*. Newcastle: Cambridge Scholars Publishing.

van Dijken, S. (1998) *John Bowlby: His Early Life: A Biographical Journey into the Roots of Attachment*. London and New York: Free Association Books.

Westheimer, I.J. (1970) 'Changes in response of mother to child during periods of Separation.' *Social Work 27*, 1, 3–10.

Williams. E. (1964) *Capitalism and Slavery*. London: Andrew Deutsch.

Subject Index

Page numbers in *italics* refer
to figures.

Author Index